T0035249

# sheet
# pan
# chicken

CATHY ERWAY

Photographs by
Lizzie Munro

# sheet pan chicken

50 simple
and satisfying
ways to cook
dinner

TEN SPEED PRESS

California | New York

# contents

## **1**   on the fly

# 2 worth the wait

# 3 chicken sidekicks

# why the chicken crossed the sheet pan

The 1990s had the George Foreman Grill. The early 2000s were all about the Dutch oven. Today, you'd be hard-pressed to find a recipe without the words "Instant Pot" before it. These trendy, and often expensive, pieces of prized cooking equipment may tempt us every decade. But a sheet pan is eternal.

A sheet pan is for roasting at its most elemental. It's the no-nonsense industrial workhorse of the home kitchen, conveniently built to maximize your sauced and seasoned ingredients' exposure to hot air, creating bronzed surfaces and crisped bottoms. Casserole dishes, with their high sides, reduce airflow and prevent your food from browning as much as it could. Cast-iron pans, with their limited real estate, can only handle a small crowd. But shallow, rimmed sheet pans make efficient use of your oven space and your time, delivering everything from bronze-topped vegetables to crisped potatoes and chickpeas to umami-blessed roasted chicken. And it can be all yours for less than $30.

As the world's second-biggest fan of chicken (the number one fan being my terrier mutt, Doug), I love it unconditionally, in all its forms. I love white meat, dark meat, chicken hearts, chicken feet, and whole rotisserie chickens from Costco. I've never met a sauced wing I didn't like. I love a good, piping-hot fried chicken drumstick and a not-so-good leftover one, too. I love chicken almost as much as I love my mom's Chinese dumplings (and no, you can't have it both ways, because she only makes dumplings with pork). I show up to barbecues with marinated chicken to throw on the grill. And I love bringing cold chicken salad in Tupperware to a picnic—a habit that spawned a story I wrote for *TASTE* titled "The Subtle Thrills of Cold Chicken Salad," which won me a James Beard Award.

Yet these two culinary love affairs of mine—roasting in sheet pans and chicken—didn't really meet up until I was in my twenties. Growing up in New Jersey, my Taiwan-raised Chinese mom cooked pretty much everything on the stovetop—often stir-fries that crackled in a deep chef's pan. My American father, born in upstate New York, also didn't really use the oven unless it was for a Thanksgiving turkey or pies; long-simmered stews like chili were more his style. In my youth, the family oven was often used for storing cookware, like an extra cupboard.

Roasting was my solo expedition, which began as an adult in my own kitchen (a typically small New York City one, as I have lived in Brooklyn for the last sixteen years). Enriched by a community of similarly food-obsessed friends, this journey was filled with discoveries that I relished and wrote about endlessly on my blog and in my first book, *The Art of Eating In,* published in 2010. The oven, I learned, was the gateway to so many treasures. It was where kale leaves crisped to the texture and flavor of nori. Where winter squash, halved and roasted cut-side down, bled sugars like sap and softened to fudgy smears of orange. The oven was where fatty fish fillets could cook evenly while crisping at their edges, where pork shoulder could languish and fulfill its destiny as tasty, citrusy morsels of carnitas. Where almost any vegetable—carrots, broccoli, brussels sprouts, eggplant, turnips, tomatoes—becomes not just beautifully caramelized but concentrated in flavor. And where chicken skin turns from pale, gelatinous sheaths to golden brittle. That's the beauty of dry heat: zapping moisture so that the ingredients crisp and concentrate, intensifying in flavor like a tomato left in the sun to dry.

And this is the nexus of the recipes in this book: By roasting chicken on a sheet pan along with everything you want to eat with it, you have a family of ingredients that are individually intensifying in flavor while at the same time, by sheer proximity, leaching up the rendered juices and fats from the chicken, lifting up their flavors even more. Apples roasted without chicken on the same pan would be a much less exciting product (and a vegan one). Onions are not just onions once they're on a sheet pan with chicken; you're taking advantage of every droplet of the incredible flavor enhancer that is chicken fat—properly revered in traditional Jewish cooking and named schmaltz in Yiddish. And when you crisp the chicken skin, it's worthy of grabbing the spotlight as in kawa yakitori, Japanese grilled skewers of just chicken skin.

Throughout this book, you'll encounter different combinations of chicken, vegetables, grains, and spices all undergoing this metamorphosis into a higher dimension of flavor together. In some of the recipes, you'll see that those combinations were inspired by well-loved dishes that are not typically cooked on a sheet pan. They might have roots in other cooking methods, such as over an open fire, or in a big old pot, or whatever it made the most sense to cook in at the time and place the dish came into being (in the case of the New England clambake–inspired recipe on page 53, that happened to be a dug-out trench in the sand).

I'm convinced that roasting chicken is one of the easiest ways to coax out all the flavors and features chicken provides, from the sweet, sticky glaze that may form on its skin to the seasoned juices that run freely from a wingette's succulent flesh. And unlike stovetop preparations, you're not constantly tossing things around in a splattering pan. There's something so satisfying about wiping your hands and walking away from the kitchen for a good while after you've shoved a sheet pan in the oven. It's one of the few hands-off moments in cooking. Set it and forget it, as the saying goes. So as a simple, flexible route to dinner, cranking up the oven and assembling ingredients on a sheet pan makes a lot of sense for home cooks today. And it's very telling that this is a popular cooking method in *home* kitchens— rather than in restaurants, where the chef move of "picking up" (or

why the chicken crossed the sheet pan

finishing the dish) on the stovetop is more the rule than the exception. There are simply dishes and cooking practices that are well suited to home cooking, and there are those that are well suited to restaurant cooking, and these two styles do not overlap nearly as much as some cookbooks would like you to believe.

Once you know how to roast a sheet pan full of chicken and vegetables one way, you're ready to start improvising with seasonal ingredients as they hit the farmers' market. In most of these recipes, the prep work and oven time are relatively minimal, particularly in the first section, "On the Fly." But there are always extra steps and tips that can really expand your cooking IQ: to ensure that the chicken skin is crispy as can be, or that the meat is supremely marinated, or just to do something kind of funky and out there— and also delicious. So the second section, "Worth the Wait," is for those recipes that call for a longer lead time.

Most important, this cookbook gathers chicken recipes that really thrive on a sheet pan. Not every beloved dish, from every cuisine, translates well to this format. But I was delighted by the way oven-roasting some dishes, like Chinese Lion's Head Meatballs (page 39), gave them wholly new dimensions, setting them apart from the original. And some dishes were just too irresistible not to give a sheet pan spin, like Mustard Chicken with Bacon, Mushrooms, and Onions (page 73), a hearty French stew. So I've taken inspiration from favorite chicken recipes from around the world—whether they originated on the hibachi or the stovetop or anywhere else—and I've asked a handful of cookbook authors with whom I'm enamored to contribute recipes for this book, too. Each of these women has greatly helped me understand the cuisines of their heritage through their work, so I'm grateful to feature recipes from Melissa Clark, Jenn de la Vega, Von Diaz, Pati Jinich, Yewande Komolafe, Preeti Mistry, Leela Punyaratabandhu, and Louisa Shafia, as well as recipes inspired by Darra Goldstein, Sara Jenkins, and Andrea Nguyen.

Developing dozens of sheet pan chicken recipes was a dream project that I took on with the passion of a chicken with too many delicious things to peck. I am so thrilled with the results of my many experiments and the recipes of those contributors, and I hope you will be, too. This is not haute cuisine, but recipes from and for the home cook, focused on a single, chicken-y theme you can feel empowered to riff on at your will. Simple, flexible, and delicious, these are the hallmarks of a winner chicken dinner in my book.

### how did chicken win our dinner?

I'm not the only one obsessed with chicken—it's the most popular animal protein cooked in America today. But it wasn't always this way. Before 1940, Americans ate around 10 pounds of chicken per year on average. Now we eat around 95 pounds of chicken per year, according to the National Chicken Council.

That's in large part due to industrial farming systems designed to increase production to feed the country's growing population after World War II, but marketing and food science are also at work. And for more than four decades, starting in the late 1950s, Robert C. Baker, a prominent scientist at Cornell University, was tasked with developing products for all those chickens entering the market, broadening Americans' appreciation for poultry. He created chicken nuggets and poultry hot dogs, and promoted ways for home cooks to prepare chicken. His barbecue sauce for grilling chicken, now known as Cornell sauce (see page 80), didn't catch on beyond the Finger Lakes region of upstate New York, where Cornell is based. But the idea of grilling chicken with some kind of sauce—or just eating chicken more often—certainly did.

# how to choose your sheet pan

Unlike, say, teapots and sprinklers, sheet pans come in standardized sizes and have only a few variations beyond that.

Pretty much all the recipes in this book call for a rimmed half sheet pan. A true baker's half sheet pan should measure 18 by 13 inches—but sometimes, manufacturers skimp on those dimensions by a fraction of an inch here or there. Depending on the size of your oven, one pan could fit snugly on one rack when slid widthwise, or, if you have a wider oven, two pans turned lengthwise might barely fit on one rack. Full sheet pans are often too large to fit into a home oven and are reserved for commercial baking. There's also the quarter sheet pan, (13 by 9 inches), and the one-eighth pan (9 by 6 inches), which is about the right size for most toaster ovens. You might find square sheet pans or rectangular pans that look like they're in between a quarter sheet pan and a half sheet pan in size. They might be called a "jelly-roll pan," or, simply a "baking sheet." But you'll want to own at least one (and preferably two) 18 by 13-inch half sheet pan to maximize the space for your ingredients and help ensure there's enough room for them to bake and bubble to a perfect crisp. And make sure it's a commercial-grade (sometimes called "double-thick") aluminum half sheet pan with a rolled edge about 1 inch in height, high enough to keep juices from running off.

## what about a cookie sheet?

Any flat baking sheet without a rim should be reserved specifically for baked goods that don't drip, and you'll often see these labeled "cookie sheets" (although this term is sometimes used interchangeably with "sheet pan" and "baking sheet" in recipes, which can be confusing). Cookie sheets are rimless to allow even more airflow across the top of the cookies, and for supposed ease of removing said cookies from the pan. They are used often in commercial bakeries, but if you ask me, a rimless pan is unnecessary for home kitchens, since you can use a rimmed sheet pan for cookies and pastries, but your rimless cookie sheet can't do double-duty for roasting chicken. You'll also want to pass on using "insulated" baking sheets for pretty much anything besides cookies and desserts; the layer of air inside the pan is to promote more even, but softer, cooking on the bottom, and that's not what we want for our crispy, seared-bottom sheet pan meals.

## nonstick vs. non-nonstick

Roasting can be sticky business. That crusty goodness on your sheet pan can transform from golden brown to molasses black and be an incredible pain to scrub off. But I find that a good soak in soap and warm water is really all an uncoated aluminum sheet pan needs, and the big guns (heavy-duty scouring materials like steel wool) are perfectly suitable to use, since there's nothing like enamel or nonstick coating for you to worry about scraping off. Your sheet pan might acquire a funky patina over time, and that's just fine.

But if you prefer to go with nonstick just to foolproof the cleaning process, go for it. Just don't use steel wool to buff its surface when you do give it a clean, or you'll scrape off the nonstick coating, which could wind up in your next dinner.

### another great piece of equipment: the "fish spatula"

This is not a cookbook with a long list of "equipment" you need to invest in, and I'm not one to own chef-y gadgets. But a thin, flexible, slotted metal spatula commonly known as a fish spatula works like a charm for pulling browned-on-the-bottom foods cleanly away from cooking surfaces they're stuck to—like a sheet pan—while leaving the crispy goods intact. Although they're called fish spatulas for good reason—the length makes it perfect for scooping up a delicate, whole trout without its breaking—I use mine every day for perfectly pulling fried eggs off a cast-iron pan. And I find them indispensable for lifting pretty much anything off a sheet pan (unless the pan is nonstick, in which case you won't want to use a metal utensil).

## parchment paper or aluminum foil?

To ensure quicker cleanup, many people advise placing a sheet of parchment paper or aluminum foil on your sheet pan before adding your ingredients. I find that with most chicken recipes, however, these just get in the way. Aluminum foil has a way of adhering itself to crispy bits of skin (the best part) and tears easily when you try to remove it—for an unwelcome metallic surprise when encountering bits of metal. Parchment paper doesn't tear as readily, so it's the better choice for quicker cleanup. But personally, I feel that it looks kind of messy; the paper can become scorched and discolored, and it can absorb some of the precious juices from the pan, thereby robbing your meal of that flavor. In my opinion, it's not worth using in most cases, since the cleanup is so straightforward anyway.

However, I do recommend using parchment paper to cordon off sections of your sheet pan for different ingredients, so that juices from ingredients on one side don't interfere with ingredients browning on the other side. Those extra juices can stay in their section and bubble into a sauce (see Chicken Katsu with Plum Sauce, page 38).

## corrugated vs. flat

Some sheet pans have a corrugated texture or fluting across the surface, while some are utterly smooth. Both are fine to use in any recipe here. The texturing is just there to help the sheet pan maintain its structural integrity, preventing it from warping in a super-hot oven. Warping is a very important thing to prevent—it's why you want to get a heavy-duty commercial-grade or "double-thick" sheet pan in the first place. The uneven surface of a warped sheet pan will send juices rushing to one side or corner, resulting in uneven doneness and possibly even dripping onto the bottom of the oven and burning. I personally love corrugated sheet pans, because I feel that any measure to strengthen the sheet pan is a good idea; also, your sheet pan may warp over time, and corrugation can help delay that general wear and tear.

## an important note about overcrowding, consistency, and temperature

Sometimes, your head of cauliflower just yields too many little florets, or you just want to use up the rest of your potatoes. In these moments, it's much better to break out another sheet pan for those spill-over ingredients than to try to squeeze everything onto one pan just for the sake of using one pan. When you overcrowd a sheet pan, with ingredients bumping up against one another, their collective moisture will steam them rather than allowing them to roast. And if your chicken is on top of the potatoes or your ingredients are not in a single layer, then they all might take longer to cook.

That said, I am not one of those cookbook authors who will lead you to believe that ingredients are always going to behave the same way in your home oven. Consistency is a goal, but cooking is not a precise science with exact inputs—every onion or piece of chicken is unique, just like people. You might have radishes that refuse to get crispy even after roasting at 450°F for 30 minutes, because they are fresher and have a higher moisture content. (At least all ovens perform exactly the same. Psych! Of course they don't.) Adjusting is part of the art of cooking, which is why I instruct you to do things like rotate the pan and check on it after 20 minutes. And still, some ingredients won't brown the same way as they did the last time you made the same recipe, following the same steps. These things happen, so embrace the variety. And take the opportunity to use slightly past-its-prime produce for roasting, because they'll fare just fine compared to trying to enjoy them fresh in a salad.

That *and* that said, I advise getting a simple meat thermometer that costs less than $10—and get used to stabbing chicken with it for reassurance. Every piece of chicken has a unique BMI, so its temperature, the color of its flesh, and the opaqueness of its juices are really the only ways to judge whether that chicken is fully cooked—not the recipe's timing instructions.

# how to choose your chicken

When I was a high schooler in the 1990s, I became obsessed with an avant-garde rock duo called Cibo Matto and their song "Know Your Chicken." Its enigmatic chorus—"I know my chicken / You've got to know your chicken"—still rings in my head every time I peer over the fluorescent-lit refrigerated cases at the grocery store, debating which chicken to buy.

So, how do you know your chicken? Well, you can go to the farmers' market or a farm stand in your area and buy it from a person who knows your chicken pretty well. You can ask her many questions, too. Short of that, I like to look for "free-range," "pasture-raised," and "organic" on the label, although there is a whole lot of confusion out there in chicken-labeling land, as new terms get adopted and sometimes twisted to the point of meaninglessness over time. Some labels can only be used by producers if they meet certain standards— the USDA "organic" certification for chicken, for example, requires that the chickens are fed an organic diet, are given no antibiotics, and have some access to outdoor space (although exactly how much space is vague). If you see the label "Animal Welfare Approved," the chicken has been certified by AGW (A Greener World), an organization that has strict regulations for what constitutes free-range or pasture-raised. While strong animal welfare standards don't necessarily have an effect on the chicken's quality, I find that producers who invest in such certification produce a tastier bird more frequently than not. And because a chicken's diet affects the taste, texture, and color of its meat, you might see more yellowish skin and fat on birds that enjoyed eating a diet rich in beta-carotene, which they can get from grass. This is a sign that the chicken may have been allowed to graze.

"Antibiotic-free" or "no antibiotics ever" is another label that you'll see when buying chickens; forgoing the use of antibiotics when raising chickens is a practice that has been widely adopted by producers to help combat the rise of antibiotic-resistant bacteria and diseases. It's definitely a good idea to buy chicken that indicates this. Another distinction on chicken labels is whether or not it was produced using regenerative agricultural practices, a response to today's dominant industrial agriculture practices; this movement is based on finding ways to slow climate change while producing food, by regenerating the soil, encouraging biodiversity, and more. To promote biodiversity, you can also get heritage-breed chickens, which are simply breeds of chicken that haven't been factory-farmed over the past century or so. And because industrially raised chickens have been bred to have larger and larger breasts, heritage-breed chickens tend to be more lean-looking by contrast, with a greater ratio of dark meat.

Finally, you might see chicken that has been described as "air-chilled" before packing; this is a great thing to look for if you're planning on roasting the chicken. This means the chicken hasn't been submerged in liquids to chill it down during processing, which can bulk up the weight of the meat but also dilutes the flavor a bit. Air-chilling is a much slower process, and will result in a drier bird—which is exactly what you want for roasting. A drier raw bird will yield crispier, tastier results.

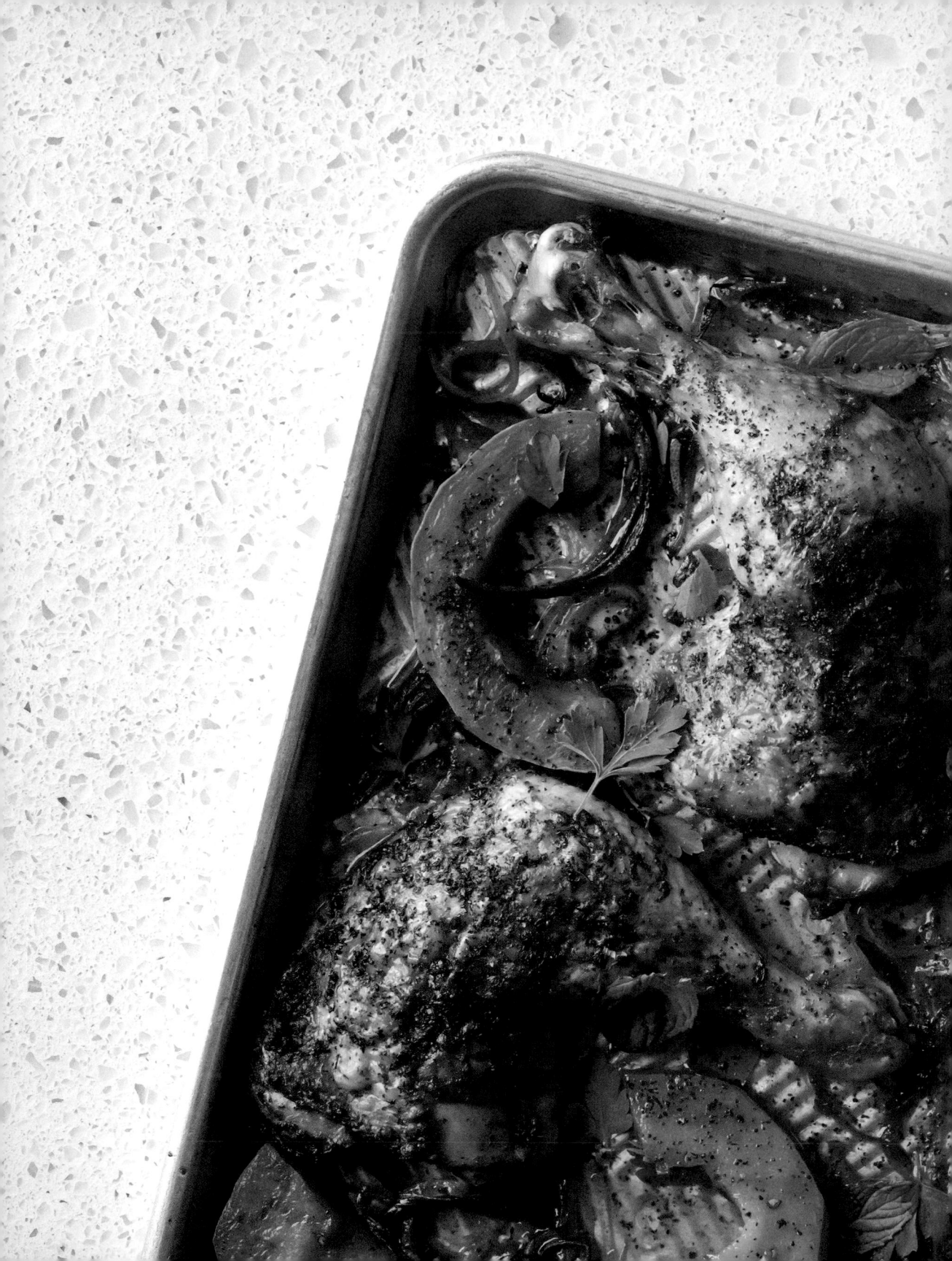

# a chicken parts chart

| part | what it is |
|---|---|
| **WHOLE CHICKEN (OFTEN CALLED A ROASTER OR YOUNG CHICKEN)** | This is the whole shebang, minus the head and feet, typically. It can be anywhere from 2 pounds to 7 or 8 pounds. |
| **WHOLE BREAST (OFTEN CALLED SPLIT CHICKEN BREAST)** | This is the skin-on, bone-in breast (a whole chicken has two breast portions; "split" refers to splitting them apart), averaging around 1 pound each. When roasted, this yields juicier white meat than boneless breasts—and you'll have the benefit of crisp, golden skin. |
| **BONELESS BREAST** | This is a whole boneless and usually skinless chicken breast half. It can become dry and tough if overcooked, or when roasted without the protection of skin. It's best to cook boneless breasts very quickly, or to marinate them well if you're roasting them to help them stay juicy. |
| **THIN-SLICED CHICKEN BREASTS** | These are boneless chicken breasts cut into thinner slabs. |

Not too long ago, you had to buy a whole chicken and cut it up, or have the butcher cut it for you. Now you're more likely to find packs of all the same chicken part in the grocery store. Let's clarify what all these parts are and explain how you can swap one for another, as many of these recipes will work well with a different part of the chicken than called for. As a rule of thumb, try to make sure your pieces are all roughly the same weight if you're cooking them together on the same pan. There is no such thing as a bad chicken part—just better and worse times for cooking with them.

## substitution tips

If a recipe calls for bone-in chicken parts but you want to do a whole chicken instead, just follow the instructions to spatchcock it (see page 24); it will typically require a slightly longer oven time, but you can increase the cut size of the vegetables to prevent them from overcooking.

If cooking whole breasts with smaller parts of the chicken, the breasts can be halved fairly easily (a heavy cleaver will help) to approximate the size of the other parts. But even bone-in breasts can easily become too dry and their sizes vary greatly, so these are best roasted on their own.

You can swap in a boneless breast for a bone-in breast if you don't mind sacrificing some juiciness and the crisp skin, but you will want to reduce the cooking time by 10 to 15 minutes.

Sure, you could butterfly a whole chicken breast and wind up with these, but these thin slices, weighing anywhere from 2 to 8 ounces, are commonly available. Because their weight is so variable, you will need to check and adjust the cooking time as needed to avoid overcooking.

## suggested recipes

- Weeknight Spatchcock Chicken with Lemon and Root Vegetables (page 24)
- Spatchcock Chicken with Ginger, Garlic, and Green Papaya (page 51)

- Bang Bang Crispy Chicken (page 27)
- The Best Warm Chicken Salad with Pan Drippings Vinaigrette (page 56)

- Chicken Satay Lettuce Wraps with Peanut Sauce and Quick Pickles (page 63)
- Blackened Chicken with Andouille Sausage, Okra, and Tomatoes (page 67)

- Chicken Katsu with Plum Sauce (page 38)
- Chicken Schnitzel with Crispy Cabbage, Potatoes, and Lemon-Caper Aioli (page 42)

continued

| part | what it is |
| --- | --- |
| LEGS | These are bone-in thigh and drumstick pieces, intact and attached. Do not confuse these with leg quarters, which include the back, or a whole quarter of a bird. |
| THIGHS | These are the bone-in, skin-on (usually) part of the chicken's leg above the drumstick. |
| BONELESS THIGHS | Thigh pieces that have been deboned and often skinned, too. |
| DRUMSTICKS | This is the tibia and fibula of the chicken, with all its meat and skin on it. |
| WINGS | These are whole wings, with the wingette, drumette, and wing tip all attached and intact. |
| PARTY WINGS | These are wings separated into two pieces: the drumette and the wingette, without the wing tips. |

| substitution tips | suggested recipes |
|---|---|
| Roast these just like you would a separated thigh or leg, but be sure to check the temp to ensure that they're fully cooked, as whole legs should take a little longer than separate leg parts. | • Chicken and Eggplant with Spiced Tomatoes (page 60)<br>• Za'atar-Rubbed Chicken with Carrots, Beets, and Labne (page 69) |
| Super moist, fatty, and flavorful, thighs are the new darling of chicken recipes, including many in this book you are reading. | • Paprika Chicken with Sweet Potatoes and a Crispy Kale Crown (page 28)<br>• Mostarda Chicken Thighs with Apricots, Fennel, and Honey (page 32) |
| Since boneless thighs are moister and more flavorful than boneless breasts, but still boneless, they're quite popular nowadays. While they are not nearly as thick and solid, they can be substituted for boneless breasts in most recipes. | • Cashew Orange Chicken with Broccoli (page 41)<br>• Tomatillo Chicken with Potatoes, Poblanos, and Sweet Corn (page 70) |
| These have all the tender, flavorful dark-meat qualities as thighs. They are comparable in size and bulk to bone-in, skin-on thighs, so you could use these along with or instead of them. | • Jamaican Ginger Beer Chicken with Squash and Brussels Sprouts (page 88)<br>• Miso-Marinated Chicken with Crispy Brussels Sprouts, Baby Turnips, and Apples (page 90) |
| You can cook whole wings along with bone-in parts like drumsticks or thighs (as you would if you were cooking a whole bird cut into parts). | • Cumin Five-Spice Chicken Wings with Sweet Potatoes and Eggplant (page 47)<br>• Dak Dori Sheet Pan Chicken (page 64) |
| Since they are a smaller size than other parts of the chicken, party wings are best cooked separately. Wings have a lot of tender cartilage from joints throughout and a greater skin-to-meat ratio, so it's good to get all that skin crispy and delicious with a sauce or glaze. | • Coconut Adobo Chicken with Crispy Radish and Bok Choy (page 78)<br>• Three-Cup Chicken Wings with Eggplant and Basil (page 105) |

# how to choose the spice that's right

Pre-ordained spice blends are convenient, but relying on these alone can put you in a bind. Garam masala or curry powder? Herbes de Provence or . . . "poultry seasoning"? Of course, anything fragrant and edible could be called poultry seasoning, and you might be surprised at how many popular spice blends share the same key spices (poultry seasoning, for instance, is merely a finer dust of many of the same dried herbs as you'd find in herbes de Provence, and I'll use both interchangeably). Unless you use those spice blends so frequently that you'll empty the bottle in a few months, it makes sense to buy a few individual herbs and spices and mix them on your own—this will ensure that you use the freshest seasonings possible. I love smearing a chicken with dry spices and herbs, but you won't get the same flavor payoff when those spices and herbs are stale. So before you buy another blend to clutter your spice drawer, check out this handy chart—it might just convince you to at least get a canister each of whole coriander and cumin seeds.

| blend name | usually includes | sometimes also includes (but is not limited to) |
| --- | --- | --- |
| **CAJUN SEASONING** | Cayenne pepper, paprika, black pepper, garlic powder, onion powder, oregano, thyme | Chile powder, red chile flakes, white pepper, filé powder |
| **CHINESE FIVE SPICE** | Cinnamon, clove, star anise, fennel seed, Sichuan peppercorn | Black pepper (in lieu of Sichuan peppercorn) |
| **CURRY POWDER** | Coriander, cumin, chile pepper, turmeric, mustard seed, cardamom, cinnamon | Nutmeg, clove, fenugreek, paprika, ginger, hing (asafetida) |
| **GARAM MASALA** | Coriander, cumin, cinnamon, cardamom, clove, ginger, nutmeg, black pepper | Chile pepper, fennel seed, fenugreek, bay leaf, mustard seed, hing (asafetida) |
| **HERBES DE PROVENCE** | Oregano, rosemary, marjoram, savory, lavender | Thyme, sage, bay leaf, fennel seed |
| **MULLING SPICES** | Cinnamon, clove, nutmeg, ginger | Cardamom, allspice, citrus peel |
| **POULTRY SEASONING** | Oregano, rosemary, sage, marjoram, thyme, ginger | Black pepper, nutmeg |
| **RAS EL HANOUT** | Coriander, cumin, cinnamon, clove, ginger, chile pepper, black pepper | Turmeric, paprika, allspice, nutmeg, fennel seed, rose petal, mace |
| **TACO SEASONING** | Chile powder, cayenne pepper, cumin, coriander, oregano | Garlic powder, onion powder, paprika |
| **ZA'ATAR** | Oregano, marjoram, thyme, sesame seed, sumac | Fennel, mint, cumin, coriander, chickpea flour |

# 1

# on the fly

I tend to think of filling a sheet pan to the brim with cut vegetables and spiced and marinated chicken pieces as making one big, lazy stir-fry. But instead of stirring, the ingredients are left to roast, sweating juices and shrinking as they concentrate in flavor. This (mostly) hands-off bliss while you wait for the golden reveal can be used to tackle a few other things—like doing the laundry or retrieving all the dog toys from under the furniture. The recipes in this section have been created to be quick and simple, championing instant seasonings rather than overnight marinades. It's my hope that with the recipes in this section, you can get a feel for the rhythms and wisdom of roasting chicken with many types of ingredients—like alternative winter squashes, root vegetables, juicy fruits, and alliums—and feel empowered to wing it with other ingredients that come your way.

# weeknight spatchcock chicken
## with lemon and root vegetables

It might sound newfangled and a little funky, but spatchcocking is essentially the same thing as butterflying—and whether you're talking a whole chicken, a filet, or a leg of lamb, that means splitting it to lie flat, like an open book. For chicken, this involves cutting out the backbone first, which is the only tricky part, but for your (or your butcher's) efforts, you'll greatly reduce the time the chicken takes to cook. That's the raison d'être of spatchcocking. I'll admit, the chicken looks like it's doing some crazy yoga pose, especially with its wings tucked behind its back. (I think it's doing Fixed Firm Pose or Supta Vajrasana in Bikram yoga—just Google it.) But splayed over a sheet pan, surrounded with a few chunky potatoes and roots to absorb its juices, it'll cook beautifully—and quickly, making it weeknight-worthy. **Serves 4**

1 lemon

1 (3½-pound) whole chicken

About 1½ pounds assorted root vegetables, such as unpeeled carrots, parsnips, turnips, rutabaga, radishes, beets, or peeled celery root, or go ahead and just use peeled potatoes or sweet potatoes

2 small to medium onions, quartered

4 tablespoons extra-virgin olive oil

2½ teaspoons salt

1¼ teaspoons black pepper

2 tablespoons herbes de Provence or a combo of dried herbs like oregano, rosemary, sage, and thyme (see page 21)

About ½ cup chopped fresh flat-leaf parsley leaves or other fresh herbs (thyme, rosemary, tarragon, dill, chervil, oregano, or anything you like; optional)

Preheat the oven to 450°F.

Zest and halve the lemon and set both aside. Remove the neck and gizzards from the chicken's cavity and discard (or save them for making stock or dog treats later).

Spatchcock the chicken: place it breast-side down on a cutting board. Using kitchen scissors (if you have a cleaver or sharp chef's knife, you can use that—carefully—instead), snip along each side of the spine to remove it. Flip the chicken breast-side up, place your palm on the center of the breast, and push down until you feel the breastbone crack. This should help the chicken lie flat. Gently slide your finger underneath the skin of the breast to detach it from the meat a bit (this will encourage the skin to crisp up in the oven). Tuck the wing tips underneath the wings to prevent them from burning. Squeeze the juice from one lemon half all over the chicken's surface and set it aside to dry a bit while you prepare the rest of the ingredients.

Wash and dry the root vegetables well and cut them into 1-inch chunks. Combine the vegetables, onions, 2 tablespoons of the olive oil, ½ teaspoon of the salt, and ¼ teaspoon of the pepper on a sheet pan and spread them in an even layer.

Rub the remaining 2 teaspoons salt and 1 teaspoon pepper all over the skin and the underside of the chicken. Rub just the skin with the remaining 2 tablespoons olive oil and the herbes de Provence. Place the chicken skin-side up on top of the vegetables on the sheet pan. Roast until a kitchen thermometer inserted into the thickest part of a thigh registers 160°F, 40 to 50 minutes, rotating the pan every 20 minutes and tossing the veggies around in the pan if they are becoming too crisp in some parts.

Remove the pan from the oven. Squeeze the remaining lemon half all over the chicken and vegetables, sprinkle with the lemon zest and fresh herbs (if using) and serve.

# bang bang crispy chicken

Sichuan cuisine is all about bringing big flavors—with dishes like kou shui ji, or "mouth-watering chicken" (sometimes translated as "saliva chicken" because of the way its numbing-hot spices make you drool) and guawei ji, or "strange flavor chicken" (again, a literal description of its curiously delicious spices). Another amazingly named chicken dish from China's Sichuan Province is "bang bang chicken" (sometimes translated as "bon bon chicken"), but this time, the name describes the wooden stick used to bang on the chicken after it's been cooked. Why bang on the chicken? It will help you quickly tear the chicken into delicate shreds. That shredded meat is placed in a serving dish, and a tangy, spicy, and slightly sweet sauce is poured over it, working its way into all the nooks and crannies and getting totally absorbed by the chicken. Bang Bang Chicken is typically made with poached or steamed chicken breasts. And sure, you could substitute boneless, skinless chicken breasts here, but I'd recommend any bone-in, skin-on chicken pieces, so you'll get crispy skin as well as juicy meat and drippings to add to your sauce. **Serves 3 or 4**

2 bone-in, skin-on chicken breasts or any other bone-in, skin-on piece

1 tablespoon toasted sesame oil

1 teaspoon salt

½ teaspoon white pepper

**for the sauce**

2 tablespoons Crispy Chile Oil (page 128), or more to taste

1 tablespoon Chinese sesame paste (optional)

1 teaspoon toasted sesame oil

¼ cup soy sauce

¼ cup Chinese black vinegar or red wine vinegar

2 tablespoons sugar

1 (1-inch) piece fresh ginger, peeled and julienned

Steamed rice; cooked Asian wheat noodles, soba noodles, or bean thread noodles; or shredded lettuce for serving

1 medium cucumber, peeled, seeded, and julienned

½ cup roasted peanuts, coarsely chopped (optional)

2 scallions, thinly sliced on a bias

1 cup cilantro leaves and tender stems, coarsely chopped

Preheat the oven to 450°F.

Rub the chicken with the sesame oil, salt, and white pepper. Gently slide your finger underneath the skin of each breast to loosen it from the meat a bit (this will encourage the skin to crisp up in the oven). Place the chicken on a sheet pan, skin-side up. Roast for 30 to 35 minutes, until the chicken skin is nicely crisped and a kitchen thermometer inserted into a breast registers 160°F.

Meanwhile, make the sauce: In a small bowl, combine the chile oil, optional sesame paste, sesame oil, soy sauce, vinegar, sugar, and ginger. Set aside.

Transfer the pan to a flat surface—one that's heat-proof or protected with hot pads. Slowly press down on each chicken piece with a rolling pin and roll along its length so the meat breaks and shreds apart a bit. If preferred, remove and discard the bones. Scrape the pan to collect any browned bits and juices and add them to your sauce.

Place the rice, noodles, or shredded lettuce in a large serving dish and set the banged-up chicken pieces on top; otherwise, put the chicken directly in the serving dish. Scatter the cucumber over the chicken, then pour the sauce all over. Top with the peanuts (if using), scallions, and cilantro and enjoy.

# paprika chicken
## with sweet potatoes and a crispy kale crown

Whenever I smell chicken paprikash or goulash, two warhorse Central European stews, I'm taken back to playing in my backyard at dusk. Growing up, my next-door neighbors were an elderly Polish couple, and an intoxicatingly savory, spicy, and slightly smoky smell would waft into our yard from their house around dinnertime— a smell that I'm now convinced came from chicken steeping in paprika. To be honest, I think there could be a whole cookbook devoted to chicken and paprika recipes alone (like the Pimentón Chicken on page 66), so a chicken paprikash stew translated for cooking on a sheet pan was one of the first ideas I rushed to create for this book. I've given it some nontraditional accents with sweet potatoes and a crispy kale crown—a canopy of oiled leaves draped over the whole sheet pan. The crispy kale can actually be applied to just about any other recipe during the last 15 minutes of cooking, so I've included it as a bonus recipe here (see photo on pages 30–31). And since chicken paprikash stews are enriched with sour cream for thickness and dairy tang, I've included an optional sour cream–based sauce to serve on the side. **Serves 3 or 4**

1½ to 2 pounds bone-in, skin-on chicken pieces, such as thighs or legs

1 garlic clove, grated or minced

3 teaspoons sweet paprika

2 teaspoons salt

About 3 tablespoons extra-virgin olive oil

1½ pounds sweet potatoes

2 cubanelle or bell peppers (any color), cut into long slivers about ½ inch thick

1 medium onion, halved through the root and sliced crosswise ½ inch thick

Crispy Kale Crown (recipe follows)

Paprika Sauce (optional; recipe follows)

Preheat the oven to 425°F.

In a large bowl, combine the chicken, garlic, 2 teaspoons of the paprika, 1 teaspoon of the salt, and about 1 tablespoon of the olive oil.

Quarter the sweet potatoes lengthwise, then slice the quarters lengthwise into evenly sized triangular spears no thicker than 1 inch wide (depending on how large your sweet potatoes are, you may end up cutting them into eighths or sixteenths). In a large bowl, toss the sweet potatoes, cubanelles, and onion with the remaining 2 tablespoons olive oil, 1 teaspoon salt, and 1 teaspoon paprika.

Arrange the sweet potato wedges on a sheet pan, spacing them so that no two are touching and leaving some room for the chicken. Arrange the chicken pieces on the pan. Scatter the peppers and onion around and in between the sweet potato and chicken. Roast for 30 minutes.

Add the kale crown and roast for another 10 to 15 minutes, until a kitchen thermometer inserted into the thickest part close to the bone registers 160°F.

Just before serving, quickly reheat the sauce (if using) and pour it into a bowl or gravy boat. Serve the chicken and vegetables with the warm sauce on the side.

# crispy kale crown

Try adding this crispy kale to any recipe that calls for roasting chicken at 400° to 450°F.

4 curly kale leaves, stripped of thick ribs

1 tablespoon extra-virgin olive oil

¼ teaspoon salt

Rub the kale leaves with the olive oil and salt. When the chicken has 15 minutes left to roast, drape the kale pieces over the whole sheet pan, in as even a layer as you can, and return the pan to the oven to roast for another 10 to 15 minutes, until the chicken is cooked through and the kale is gently browned on the edges.

# paprika sauce

1 tablespoon extra-virgin olive oil

1 tablespoon tomato paste

¾ cup chicken stock

¼ cup sour cream

Pinch of sweet paprika

Pinch of dried thyme

Salt and black pepper

Heat the olive oil in a small saucepan over medium-high heat. Add the tomato paste and stir for about 30 seconds, until warm. Add the stock and whisk to blend. Bring to a boil, then reduce the heat to maintain a simmer. Whisk in the sour cream and bring the sauce to a low boil. Add the paprika and thyme, and season with salt and pepper. Taste for seasoning and add more salt and pepper as desired. Remove from the heat until you're ready to serve.

# mostarda chicken thighs
## with apricots, fennel, and honey

Dried apricots deserve your respect. Soft and squishy, sweet and wrinkly, they are the best kind of dried fruit, and their virtues have been exploited in many sauces around the world, from Chinese American duck sauce to Moroccan tagines with lamb to the tangy condiment mostarda. Mostarda, with roots in the northern Italian region of Emilia-Romagna, comes in many forms and might be confused for just mustard—but mustard it is not. Commonly prepared as a sort of jam or chutney of dried fruits cooked in mustard and vinegar and studded with vibrant orange dried apricots, it is often served with a cheese board. (The Basque restaurant that catered my wedding served mostarda, and I couldn't get enough of it.) I've built in a jammy sort-of-mostarda toward the end of cooking this chicken and fennel. The distinct anise and mint flavors marry with the crisped chicken and its plentiful juices, while the apricots and vinegar make for the perfect balance of savory and sweet.

**Serves 4 to 6**

6 bone-in, skin-on chicken thighs

2 to 3 tablespoons extra-virgin olive oil

1½ teaspoons salt

½ teaspoon black pepper

Pinch of cayenne pepper

1 large fennel bulb

1 small red onion or shallot, thinly sliced

10 dried apricots, thinly sliced

½ cup white wine vinegar

2 tablespoons honey

1 tablespoon whole-grain mustard

¼ cup fresh mint leaves, torn or coarsely chopped (optional)

Preheat the oven to 450°F.

Drizzle the chicken with 1 tablespoon of the olive oil and season with 1 teaspoon of the salt, ¼ teaspoon of the black pepper, and the cayenne. Arrange the chicken around the edges of a sheet pan.

Trim the stalks and fronds from the fennel bulb; coarsely chop about ¼ cup of fresh-looking fronds and set aside for garnish. (Save any fennel stalks and extra fronds for making stock another time.) Halve the fennel bulb crosswise and slice it into thin half rings about ¼ inch thick. Toss the fennel in the center of the sheet pan with the remaining 1 to 2 tablespoons olive oil, ½ teaspoon salt, and ¼ teaspoon black pepper. Roast for 20 minutes.

Meanwhile, combine the onion, apricots, vinegar, honey, and mustard in a medium bowl and mix well. Pour the apricot mixture all over the fennel. Roast for another 15 to 20 minutes, until the chicken skin is nicely browned and a kitchen thermometer inserted into the thickest part of a thigh registers 160°F.

Garnish with the fennel fronds and mint leaves, if desired, and serve.

# stuffed peppers, kofta-style
## with tahini-yogurt sauce

Kofta (or kefta) are the meatballs or meat loaf of Central and South Asia and the Middle East. Whether the meat mixture is made with ground beef, lamb, chicken, or fish and stretched with bulgur, rice, or bread crumbs, it's always got a good kick of warming spices. Kofta are often shaped into balls or around skewers for grilling, but I've applied this concept to stuffed peppers, a pretty retro American dining concept (I think the last time I heard about stuffed peppers was in an episode of *The Golden Girls*). I like the flavor the roasted bell pepper adds to the kofta, but you could use it to fill a scooped-out zucchini, summer squash, or eggplant instead. There's enough room left on the sheet pan that you can make a lot of crispy kale rather than just draping a crown of kale over it all (see page 29). And go all Jackson Pollock with the tahini-yogurt sauce at the end—it makes a refreshing contrast. **Serves 4**

1 pound ground chicken

2 tablespoons rendered chicken or duck fat (optional)

½ cup cooked bulgur or rice

⅓ cup walnuts, chopped (optional)

2 scallions, chopped, or ⅓ cup chopped onion

2 large garlic cloves, minced or grated

¼ cup fresh mint leaves, chopped, plus more for garnish, or 1 teaspoon dried oregano

1 teaspoon salt, plus more as needed

½ teaspoon ground cumin

½ teaspoon paprika (smoked paprika is good, too)

¼ teaspoon black pepper, plus more as needed

¼ teaspoon red chile flakes

¼ teaspoon ground allspice

¼ teaspoon cayenne pepper (optional, if you like it a little spicier)

1 egg, beaten

2 large bell peppers (any color)

4 tablespoons extra-virgin olive oil

6 to 8 kale leaves, thick ribs stripped

½ cup Good on Everything Tahini-Yogurt Sauce (page 124)

Preheat the oven to 425°F.

Combine the ground chicken, rendered fat (if using), bulgur, walnuts (if using), scallions, half of the garlic, the mint, salt, cumin, paprika, black pepper, chile flakes, allspice, cayenne (if using), and egg in a large bowl and mix thoroughly with your hands to combine.

Halve each bell pepper lengthwise and carefully pull out the stem and white membrane with your hands. Shake out the seeds. Rub the pepper halves all over with 2 tablespoons of the olive oil and sprinkle with a little salt. Stuff each pepper half with the meat mixture and place them on a sheet pan, cut-side up. Roast for 30 minutes.

Meanwhile, rub the kale leaves with the remaining 2 tablespoons olive oil and season with a couple pinches of salt and black pepper.

After 30 minutes, remove the sheet pan from the oven and scatter the kale around the pan. Raise the oven temperature to 450°F and return the sheet pan to the oven. Roast for about 10 minutes more, until the kale is very crisp and the peppers appear wrinkly and softened.

Drizzle the tahini-yogurt sauce over the stuffed peppers and serve.

on the fly

# coriander-crusted chicken
## with crispy chickpeas and pomegranate

Skin-on chicken doesn't need a whole lot of seasoning besides salt to roast into a magazine-worthy crisp golden shell. But sometimes it's really fun to give it a *whole lot* of seasoning in addition to that simple rub of salt (or to replace the crust and flavor you'd get from the skin, if you want to use boneless, skinless breasts). This changes the texture game completely. I've crushed up whole spices and sesame seeds to create a coarse, grainy surface for the chicken–if you're using boneless cuts, you'll get some crust on top in lieu of that skin. Combined with crispy chickpeas and juicy bursts from the pomegranate seeds as a finishing surprise, this is like a Simone Biles floor routine of flavor and texture: a perfect ten. **Serves 3 or 4**

1 tablespoon coriander seeds

1 teaspoon whole black peppercorns

1 teaspoon cumin seeds

1 tablespoon sesame seeds

1½ to 2 pounds bone-in, skin-on chicken thighs or breasts or boneless, skinless thighs or breasts

4 to 6 tablespoons extra-virgin olive oil

2 teaspoons salt, plus a pinch

½ head cauliflower, cut into florets (about 4 cups; see Note)

1 cup canned chickpeas, drained and rinsed

1 lemon, halved

Crispy Kale Crown (page 29; optional)

½ cup pomegranate seeds

¼ cup pomegranate molasses (or use the juice of ½ lemon, if you can't find the molasses)

¼ cup fresh mint leaves, coarsely chopped

**NOTE** If you're using boneless chicken, cut your cauliflower florets into smaller pieces, halving or quartering them lengthwise so that no pieces are thicker than 1 inch. If you're using bone-in chicken, you can leave the florets in larger, uniformly sized pieces.

Preheat the oven to 450°F.

Combine the coriander seeds, peppercorns, and cumin seeds in a dry saucepan and toast over high heat, shaking the pan around continuously, for 1 to 2 minutes, until very fragrant. Immediately transfer the seeds to a spice grinder or a mortar and grind or crush them very coarsely. Transfer the spice mixture to a small bowl and stir in the sesame seeds.

Coat the chicken pieces with about 1 tablespoon of the olive oil and season with 1 teaspoon of the salt. Place the crushed spices on a flat plate. Press the skin or top of the chicken piece against the spices to adhere and create a spice crust. Arrange the chicken, spice crust up, on a sheet pan.

Toss the cauliflower florets in a large bowl with 1 to 2 tablespoons of the olive oil and 1 teaspoon of the salt. Scatter the cauliflower in between the chicken pieces on the pan. In the same bowl,

toss the chickpeas with the remaining 1 to 2 tablespoons of olive oil and remaining pinch of salt and scatter them over the pan. Roast for 20 minutes, then rotate the sheet pan and toss the cauliflower. Add the lemon halves cut side-down to the pan. Roast for another 15 to 20 minutes (or just 5 to 10 minutes more, if using boneless chicken), until the tops of the chicken pieces are browned and a kitchen thermometer inserted into the thickest part close to a bone registers 160°F. If adding a Crispy Kale Crown, prepare the kale according to instructions on page 29 and add it during the last 10 to 15 minutes of roasting.

Scatter the pomegranate seeds over the pan, drizzle with the pomegranate molasses, shower with the mint, and serve.

# internet chicken
## with apples, bacon, and brussels sprouts

*TASTE* founding editor Matt Rodbard and his wife, Tamar Anitai, have been making a version of a semi-viral BuzzFeed sheet pan chicken recipe for years and years. The dish, with an autumn-ish union of root vegetables, apples, and bacon, is certainly not for autumn only. It's a year-round staple in their household, and they really unlocked the sheet pan chicken secret when, one night, they added pomegranate molasses to the mix for a burst of sweetness and acidity. This turned out to be a very good decision. **Serves 4**

4 tablespoons extra-virgin olive oil

2 tablespoons red wine vinegar

2 tablespoons pomegranate molasses

2 garlic cloves, minced

1 tablespoon minced fresh rosemary

1 tablespoon minced fresh thyme

4 bone-in, skin-on chicken thighs

Salt and black pepper

1 large sweet potato, peeled and coarsely chopped into ¾-inch pieces

8 to 10 brussels sprouts, halved

2 medium Fuji apples, cored and sliced into half-moons about ¾ inch thick

6 to 8 slices smoked bacon, chopped crosswise into 1-inch-wide pieces

Preheat the oven to 450°F.

In a large bowl, combine 2 tablespoons of the olive oil, the vinegar, pomegranate molasses, garlic, rosemary, and thyme. Add the chicken and season with salt and pepper. Massage the chicken with your hands (both of them!), working to distribute the herbs and seasoning evenly over the chicken. Set aside to rest at room temperature while you prepare the rest of the ingredients.

Place the sweet potato, brussels sprouts, and apples on a sheet pan. Drizzle with the remaining 2 tablespoons olive oil, then toss to evenly coat and season with salt and pepper. Spread in an even layer, turning the brussels sprouts cut-side down to get as much contact with the pan as possible.

Place the chicken thighs over the vegetable-apple mix. Scatter the chopped bacon over everything. Roast for about 30 minutes, until the chicken is well browned on top and a kitchen thermometer inserted into the thickest part of a thigh registers 160°F. Serve!

# chicken katsu
## with plum sauce

Katsu is the iconic breaded cutlet of Japan, similar to schnitzel (see page 42) but also dancing to its own DJ. While it can be served with any kind of sauce, the legendary—and highly specific—katsu sauce is a thick and tangy mixture usually involving Worcestershire sauce, soy sauce, ketchup, sugar, and vinegar. You can buy bottled katsu sauce at Asian groceries, where the most popular brand is called Bulldog. Everybody needs some Bulldog in their fridge, but you can also make katsu sauce yourself. Mine is a fruit-forward plum sauce using fresh black plums, which bubbles on the same sheet pan as the chicken. The key here is to cordon off a section of your sheet pan using a folded sheet of parchment paper as a divider to keep the plum sauce separate from the chicken as it cooks. And feel free to scratch that creative itch and make an origami bowl with a sheet of parchment paper, if you can. **Serves 4**

½ cup all-purpose flour

1 egg, lightly beaten

¼ cup water

1 cup panko bread crumbs

1½ teaspoons salt

¾ teaspoon white pepper

4 pieces thin-sliced chicken breast, or 2 boneless, skinless whole breasts, butterflied and split

1 pound sugar snap peas

1 tablespoon neutral oil, such as grapeseed

**for the plum sauce**

3 black plums, pitted and diced

1 small onion or large shallot, finely diced (about ½ cup)

1 tablespoon soy sauce

1 tablespoon sugar

2 tablespoons rice vinegar

1 teaspoon Worcestershire sauce or fish sauce

¼ teaspoon dry mustard powder, or a dab of Dijon mustard

¼ teaspoon salt

1 teaspoon cornstarch

Preheat the oven to 450°F. Tear off a piece of parchment paper that's longer than your sheet pan by 3 to 4 inches. Fold one-third of the length of the parchment paper over itself, then make another fold 1 inch from the folded edge. Fit the parchment onto the sheet pan so the folded edge forms a 1-inch-high divider across the pan.

Place the flour on a plate. Whisk together the egg and water in a shallow dish. Place the panko on a separate plate and mix with ½ teaspoon of the salt and ¼ teaspoon of the white pepper.

Sprinkle both sides of the chicken slices with ½ teaspoon of the salt and ¼ teaspoon of the white pepper. Working with one piece of chicken at a time, dredge each slice in the flour and shake off any excess, then dip it in the egg wash, letting any excess drip off. Dredge in the panko mixture, coating the slice completely, then place the breaded chicken on the parchment-covered side of the sheet pan. Roast for 10 minutes.

Meanwhile, toss the sugar snap peas, neutral oil, and the remaining ½ teaspoon salt and ¼ teaspoon white pepper in a large bowl.

Make the plum sauce: In a medium bowl, whisk together the plums, onion, soy sauce, sugar, vinegar, Worcestershire sauce, mustard, salt, and cornstarch.

Remove the sheet pan from the oven. Pour the sauce over the sectioned-off unlined portion of the pan. Scatter the sugar snap peas around the chicken. Roast for 10 to 15 minutes, until the sauce is bubbling and the chicken is just golden brown. Serve the katsu and snap peas with the sauce on the side or drizzled on the chicken.

# chinese lion's head meatballs

In Shanghai, comfort food comes in the form of oversize meatballs braised with napa cabbage. This is the land of shih tzu tou, or lion's head meatballs, but in reality, they're enjoyed in home kitchens throughout China—and soon in your own home kitchen, too. These giant balls of ground meat—more like the size of a baseball than an actual lion's head—are usually made from pork, but the recipe works great with ground chicken, too, especially if you have some rendered chicken or duck fat to add to the mixture. (Ask your butcher for the hookup.) And instead of cooking them in a soupy braise, roasting the meatballs with a huge pile of shredded cabbage and other veggies (daikon radish and meaty mushrooms work great) gives you a supremely juicy and flavorful mass of veggies with the benefit of slightly browned, crisp edges. Serve them with steamed rice or a bowl of noodles. **Serves 3 or 4**

1 pound ground chicken

2 tablespoons rendered chicken or duck fat (optional, but recommended)

4 ounces water chestnuts, chopped

4 scallions, chopped

1 tablespoon grated fresh ginger

1 teaspoon cornstarch

1 teaspoon salt

1 teaspoon white pepper

1 teaspoon toasted sesame oil

About 1 pound napa cabbage (½ head), shredded

About ½ pound daikon radish or carrots, halved lengthwise and thinly sliced on a bias

About 6 shiitake mushrooms, stems trimmed, halved

3 tablespoons neutral oil, such as grapeseed

Cooked rice or noodles for serving

Preheat the oven to 450°F.

Combine the ground chicken, rendered fat (if using), water chestnuts, half of the chopped scallions, the ginger, cornstarch, ½ teaspoon of the salt, ½ teaspoon of the white pepper, and sesame oil in a large bowl and mix lightly using your hands; don't overwork the mixture, or it may become tough. (The meat mixture can be covered and refrigerated until you're ready to cook the meatballs, up to 2 days.) Divide and shape the meat mixture into 4 balls and place them on a sheet pan.

In a large bowl, combine the napa cabbage, daikon, mushrooms, neutral oil, and the remaining ½ teaspoon salt and ½ teaspoon white pepper and toss to coat. Spread the vegetables over the sheet pan in between and around the meatballs. Roast for 30 to 40 minutes, until the cabbage is lightly crisped at the edges and softened, rotating the pan and giving the vegetables a quick toss once midway through the cooking time.

Scatter the remaining scallions over the pan and serve with rice or noodles.

# cashew orange chicken
## with broccoli

I have mixed feelings about most American Chinese food (think takeout counter staples like General Tso's and sesame chicken). Maybe that's because I'm literally mixed—Chinese and American—and when I was growing up, my family turned up their noses at dishes that streaked fried chunks of chicken with a vapid, sweet-and-sour-ish sauce. But all around me, people (including my friends) were loving it. Years ago, curious, I created a takeout-inspired rendition of orange chicken at home, which tasted great, thanks to a fresh orange juice–based sauce, but it was a splattery mess to deep-fry the chicken pieces. On a sheet pan, you can roast chunks of marinated boneless thighs, which stay juicy and crisp thanks to a light coating of sweet potato starch, before drenching them with that OJ sauce. With some broccoli and cashews to go along with it, it might be inspired by a few other favorite Chinese takeout chicken classics—cashew chicken, orange chicken, chicken with broccoli—but whatever it is, I thoroughly enjoy it. **Serves 3 or 4**

1 to 1½ pounds boneless chicken thighs, cut into 1-inch cubes (it's okay if they're totally irregular shapes)

1 tablespoon soy sauce

1 teaspoon toasted sesame oil

1 teaspoon salt

½ teaspoon white pepper

1 large head of broccoli, cut into florets

2 tablespoons neutral oil, such as grapeseed

Salt and black pepper

½ cup sweet potato starch (optional, for creating a crispy crust on the chicken; this can be found in Asian groceries)

**for the sauce**

1 tablespoon neutral oil, such as grapeseed

1 teaspoon minced fresh ginger

1 teaspoon minced garlic

¼ teaspoon red chile flakes

1 teaspoon orange zest

½ cup fresh orange juice (from about 2 oranges)

1 teaspoon sugar

1 tablespoon soy sauce

½ cup cold water

1 teaspoon cornstarch or potato starch

1 teaspoon toasted sesame oil (optional)

1 cup unsalted roasted cashews

2 scallions, chopped

Toasted sesame seeds (optional) for serving

Steamed rice (optional) for serving

Preheat the oven to 450°F.

In a large bowl, combine the chicken, soy sauce, sesame oil, ½ teaspoon of the salt, and ¼ teaspoon of the white pepper. Toss the broccoli with the neutral oil and the remaining ½ teaspoon salt and ¼ teaspoon white pepper on a sheet pan and roast for 10 minutes.

If using the sweet potato starch, spread it over a plate and lightly dredge each piece of chicken in the starch, shaking off any excess. Place the chicken on the pan in a single layer, in between the broccoli. Roast for 5 to 7 minutes, until

the broccoli is crisp-tender and the chicken is golden-brown on the bottom.

Meanwhile, make the sauce: Combine the neutral oil, ginger, and garlic in a small saucepan and heat over high heat for a minute. Add the chile flakes, orange zest, orange juice, sugar, and soy sauce and bring to a boil.

In a small bowl, whisk together the cold water and cornstarch. Pour in the orange juice mixture and stir until it thickens. Stir in the sesame oil (if using). Drizzle the sauce, cashews, scallions, and sesame seeds (if using) over the sheet pan and serve with steamed rice, if desired.

# chicken schnitzel
## with crispy cabbage, potatoes, and lemon-caper aioli

Made with pounded and breaded cuts of boneless pork, veal, or chicken, schnitzel is the crispy cutlet of Austria and Germany—though near-identical versions are enjoyed around the globe, in fast-food sandwiches or atop bowls of noodles (see Chicken Katsu with Plum Sauce, page 38). While pan-frying or even deep-frying is the typical gateway to a crispy schnitzel, this oven-baked version saves you the mess—and unmitigated stress—of a splattering pan of oil in a tight cooking space. Also, I don't see the need to pound out the chicken since you can get thin-sliced chicken breasts (or butterfly a whole breast to get two thin pieces), which will cook quickly in the oven. Panko bread crumbs are a key here—these chunky flakes of Japanese milk bread tend to give crispier results than homemade bread crumbs or the finer crumbs found at the grocery store. Wedges of cabbage—which frizzle to a chiplike consistency at the edges—and crispy smashed potatoes are perfect (and slightly Teutonic) sides. **Serves 4**

Extra-virgin olive oil

1 pound baby red potatoes (1 to 2 inches in diameter), halved

1 pound green, red, or savoy cabbage (about ½ head), cut into about 1-inch-thick wedges

3 to 4 teaspoons salt, plus more as needed

1 teaspoon black pepper, plus more as needed

1 egg, beaten

¼ cup water

½ cup flour

1 cup panko bread crumbs

4 pieces thin-sliced chicken breast, or 2 whole boneless, skinless breasts, butterflied and split

**for the aioli**

1 egg yolk

2 garlic cloves, grated

½ teaspoon Dijon mustard

Salt

½ cup extra-virgin olive oil

½ teaspoon lemon zest plus 1 tablespoon lemon juice

1 tablespoon capers, roughly chopped

Preheat the oven to 425°F.

Drizzle about 2 tablespoons olive oil over a sheet pan and arrange the potatoes and cabbage on the pan in a single layer. (If you need more space to arrange it all flat, place extra cabbage wedges on a second sheet pan, drizzle with oil, and season with salt and pepper.) Drizzle another couple of tablespoons of olive oil over the vegetables and sprinkle evenly with 2 teaspoons of the salt and the pepper. Roast for 15 minutes and remove the pan from the oven.

Meanwhile, whisk together the egg and water in a wide, shallow bowl. Place the panko on a plate, season with a generous pinch each of salt and pepper, and stir to combine. Place the flour on another plate, season with a generous pinch each of salt and pepper, and stir to combine. Arrange the flour, egg, and panko next to each other on your counter.

Dredge a slice of chicken breast in the flour to coat, shaking off any excess, then dip it in the egg and let any excess drip off. Dredge it in the panko to coat completely, then place the breaded chicken on the sheet pan, nestled among the potatoes and cabbage. Repeat with the remaining slices of chicken. Drizzle 1 to 2 tablespoons olive oil over everything on the pan and return the pan to the oven. Increase the oven temperature to 450°F and roast for another 20 to 25 minutes, until the chicken is crispy and golden.

Meanwhile, make the aioli: Whisk the egg yolk, garlic, Dijon, and a pinch of salt in a small bowl. Drizzle in a few drops of the olive oil while whisking, then slowly drizzle in the remaining oil. Whisk in the lemon zest, lemon juice, and capers. Serve the aioli on the side.

# harissa chicken
## with potatoes and leeks

It would be wrong to talk about sheet pan chicken recipes without applauding Melissa Clark, who has written so many beloved and pioneering iterations of them. Melissa is a legendary chicken tastemaker of Colonel Sanders stature or greater (can we make a Mount Rushmore for chicken benefactors, with Clark as Lincoln? And Kenny Rogers standing in for Theodore Roosevelt, perhaps?), and I have had a huge girl crush on her since before that term went in and out of style. Her 2017 cookbook *Dinner: Changing the Game* included this garlicky, yogurt-y, harissa-drenched sheet pan chicken, and she graciously contributed the recipe, which highlights the North African roasted-red-pepper-and-chile condiment harissa, to this cookbook. **Serves 3 or 4**

1½ pounds bone-in, skin-on chicken thighs and drumsticks

1¼ pounds Yukon Gold potatoes, peeled and cut into 1-inch chunks

3 teaspoons salt

¾ teaspoon black pepper

2 tablespoons harissa

½ teaspoon ground cumin

4½ tablespoons extra-virgin olive oil, plus more as needed

2 leeks, white and light green parts only, halved lengthwise, rinsed, and thinly sliced into half-moons

½ teaspoon lemon zest

⅓ cup plain yogurt, preferably whole-milk (if using Greek yogurt, thin it with a little milk to make it drizzleable)

1 small garlic clove

1 cup mixed soft fresh herbs, such as dill, parsley, mint, and/or cilantro leaves

Fresh lemon juice

Combine the chicken and potatoes in a large bowl. Season them with 2½ teaspoons of the salt and ½ teaspoon of the pepper. In a small bowl, whisk together the harissa, cumin, and 3 tablespoons of the olive oil. Pour this mixture over the chicken and potatoes, and toss to combine. Let it stand at room temperature for 30 minutes.

Meanwhile, in a medium bowl, combine the leeks, lemon zest, ¼ teaspoon of the salt, and the remaining 1½ tablespoons olive oil.

Preheat the oven to 425°F.

Arrange the chicken and potatoes in a single layer on a sheet pan and roast for 20 minutes. Then toss the potatoes lightly and scatter the leeks over the sheet pan. Roast until the chicken is cooked through and everything is golden and slightly crisped, 20 to 25 minutes longer.

While the chicken cooks, place the yogurt in a small bowl. Grate the garlic clove over the yogurt, and season with the remaining ¼ teaspoon salt and ¼ teaspoon pepper. Spoon the yogurt over the chicken and vegetables on the baking sheet (or you can transfer everything to a platter if you want to be fancy about it). Scatter the herbs over the yogurt, drizzle some olive oil and lemon juice over the top, and serve.

# georgian garlic chicken
## with asparagus and creamy walnut sauce

Ground nuts are an excellent substitute for the richness of dairy in sauces, with the added benefit of great texture, and this recipe, adapted from a recipe for the classic Georgian dish bazhe in Darra Goldstein's *The Georgian Feast*, is a pure nut sauce flex. Roast chicken is smothered in a garlicky walnut sauce (Creamy Georgian Walnut Sauce on page 125, which is so good I think it could be served as an optional accompaniment for any roast chicken). I've added some vegetables to the sheet pan to enjoy with that sauce, as well as to soak up some of the chicken's juices. You can feel free to substitute whatever vegetables you prefer—some cut broccoli or cauliflower, carrots, zucchini, or just some potatoes. A simple cooked grain or grain-based pilaf would make a good side (such as Quinoa Pilaf with Chickpeas and Preserved Lemon, page 110), but I also love sopping up all the garlicky chicken juices and walnut sauce with a warm flatbread or pita. **Serves 3 or 4**

1½ to 2 pounds bone-in, skin-on chicken parts (thighs, legs, breasts, or whole wings)

2 garlic cloves, grated

2 teaspoons salt

1 teaspoon black pepper

¼ teaspoon cayenne pepper

3 tablespoons extra-virgin olive oil

1 bunch asparagus (preferably very skinny spears), tough ends trimmed

1 large onion, thinly sliced

1 cup Creamy Georgian Walnut Sauce (page 125)

½ cup chopped fresh cilantro or parsley leaves, (optional)

Preheat the oven to 450°F.

Toss the chicken, garlic, salt, black pepper, and cayenne pepper with 2 tablespoons of the olive oil on a sheet pan. Place the chicken skin-side up.

Cut the asparagus spears in half on a bias to make roughly 2-inch-long pieces. In a large bowl, toss the asparagus and onion with the remaining 1 tablespoon olive oil. Arrange the vegetables around and between the chicken in a single layer. Roast for 30 minutes.

Drizzle the walnut sauce all over the chicken and vegetables, shaking the pan to distribute it evenly. Roast for another 5 minutes, until a kitchen thermometer inserted into the thickest part close to the bone registers 160°F.

Scatter the herbs (if using) all over the pan and serve.

# cumin five-spice chicken wings
## with sweet potatoes and eggplant

The union of Chinese five-spice powder and chicken wings was simply meant to be. This warm, herbal spice blend gets rubbed all over the generous skin of a wing, and when roasted over high heat, it completely soars. I loved the flavor combo in my mom's five-spice Hongxiao chicken stews when I was growing up, and while stewed wings are great if you appreciate the jellylike texture of the skin, you can instead get it nice and crispy in a hot oven. I've added a western Chinese–inspired blend of cumin with a touch of Sichuan peppercorn to the dry rub here (it may make your nose twitch just a little, which is a good thing) and crisped sweet potato and eggplant spears on the same pan. Served with a glaze to splatter over everything, this is next-level Super Bowl party snack territory. Feel free to make this using any piece of bone-in chicken, increasing the oven time and chopping your vegetables into larger pieces to accommodate that. **Serves 4**

1 teaspoon Sichuan peppercorns or black peppercorns

1¼ teaspoons cumin seeds or 1 teaspoon ground

8 whole chicken wings, or 1 to 1½ pounds bone-in, skin-on drumsticks or thighs

1½ teaspoons salt

1 teaspoon Chinese five-spice powder

1 teaspoon red chile flakes

1 garlic clove, grated

3 tablespoons neutral oil, such as grapeseed

1 pound sweet potatoes, cut into 1-inch-thick wedges

1 (½- to ¾-pound) Asian eggplant, halved lengthwise and cut into 2-inch-long segments

**for the glaze**

⅓ cup packed brown sugar

¼ cup ketchup

¼ cup water

2 tablespoons soy sauce

¼ teaspoon Chinese five-spice powder

1 tablespoon toasted sesame oil

½ cup fresh cilantro leaves and tender stems, chopped

Preheat the oven to 450°F. Separately, coarsely crush the Sichuan peppercorns and whole cumin seeds in a spice grinder or mortar and pestle.

In a large bowl, combine the wings, ½ teaspoon of the Sichuan peppercorns, 1 teaspoon of the cumin, 1 teaspoon of the salt, ½ teaspoon of the five-spice powder, ½ teaspoon of the chile flakes, the garlic, and 1 tablespoon of the neutral oil. Stir to incorporate evenly. Arrange the wings on a sheet pan.

In the same bowl, combine the sweet potatoes, eggplant, the remaining ½ teaspoon Sichuan peppercorns, ¼ teaspoon crushed cumin, ½ teaspoon salt, ½ teaspoon five-spice, ½ teaspoon chile flakes, and 2 tablespoons of the neutral oil. Toss to coat. Arrange the vegetables in a single layer between and around the wings on the sheet pan.

Roast for 15 minutes, then toss the vegetables around on the pan and flip the wings. Reduce the oven temperature to 400°F and roast for another 10 to 15 minutes.

Meanwhile, make the glaze: Combine the brown sugar, ketchup, water, soy sauce, and five-spice powder in a small pot and heat over medium heat, stirring occasionally, until it begins to bubble and the sugar dissolves. Remove from the heat and stir in the sesame oil.

Drizzle the glaze over the vegetables and wings, garnish with the cilantro, and serve.

# ras el hanout chicken
## with oranges and olives

The Moroccan spice blend ras el hanout translates to "head of the shop," and that's how shopkeepers describe their most-prized, signature spice blend; hence, it can vary greatly. But it typically contains warm, pumpkin pie spices like cinnamon and ginger along with cumin, coriander, and chile (see the spice blend chart on page 21). Regardless of the exact blend, this incredibly dynamic spice is great for chicken, especially with some piquant olives and citrus. While visiting Morocco, I learned to cook a chicken tagine with olives and preserved lemon—thank you, cooking class—and also ate so many salads while I was in the country. Morocco has many delicately spiced, cooked vegetable salads, but for this recipe I leaned into a really fresh, simple salad of juicy orange segments with olives and red onion to top off this dish. Salty, bright, a little spicy, and super fragrant, this dish tastes like it takes a lot of effort to make, but it doesn't. I'd recommend serving it with some flatbread or pita, couscous, or Quinoa Pilaf with Chickpeas and Preserved Lemon (page 110). **Serves 4**

1½ to 2 pounds bone-in, skin-on chicken parts or boneless, skinless thighs

1 teaspoon coriander seeds

1 teaspoon cumin seeds

1 teaspoon ground turmeric

1 teaspoon paprika

2 teaspoons salt

¼ teaspoon ground cinnamon

¼ teaspoon ground ginger

¼ teaspoon cayenne pepper

¼ teaspoon black pepper

2 zucchini or yellow squash, quartered lengthwise and cut into 2-inch-long pieces (or 1-inch-long pieces, if using boneless chicken)

1 red bell pepper, thinly sliced

3 tablespoons extra-virgin olive oil

2 oranges

⅓ cup mixed olives with pits (green, black, and purplish ones, but not black olives from a can or stuffed cocktail olives)

½ red onion, halved and thinly sliced

1 cup fresh cilantro or parsley leaves, coarsely chopped

Cooked couscous or flatbread or pita for serving

Preheat the oven to 450°F.

Combine the chicken, coriander, cumin, turmeric, paprika, salt, cinnamon, ginger, cayenne, black pepper, zucchini, bell pepper, and olive oil in a large bowl. Toss to combine. Spread on a sheet pan in an even layer (it's okay if the pan is a little crowded at this point). Roast for 20 minutes. Toss the vegetables around, rotate the pan, and roast for another 20 to 25 minutes if using bone-in chicken, or another 10 minutes if using boneless thighs.

Cut a slice off the bottom of each orange so they sit flat on your cutting board. Following the curve of the fruit, cut away the peel and white pith. Holding an orange over a bowl, carefully cut along the sides of each segment to free them from the membrane and allow them to fall into the bowl (these fancy, pith-free citrus segments are called suprêmes in chef-speak).

To pit the olives, working one at a time, place an olive on your cutting board and set the flat side of a chef's knife over it. Using your palm, press against the flat of the knife to squish the olive against the cutting board. The meat will break away from the pit (you can leave it in large pieces); discard the pit.

Scatter the orange segments, olives, and red onion all around on the sheet pan and garnish with the cilantro. Serve with couscous, flatbread, or pita.

# roast chicken
## with crushed fennel and citrusy red palm oil dressing

Sustainably sourced, unrefined red palm oil is a West African culinary ingredient, totally different from the refined palm oil that is used in industrial food production—and is the subject of much scorn from environmentally conscious eaters. Red palm oil (also called palm fruit oil) is a staple of Nigerian cooking, often used in soups and stews, and it's viscous, fruit-forward, and earthy at the same time. This was all explained to me by chef and recipe developer Yewande Komolafe, who cleverly developed a dressing using red palm oil for this recipe, which she contributed to this book. She says the oil is easy to find at any African market in Brooklyn, where she lives, and is also available online. **Serves 4**

1 tablespoon fennel seeds

1 tablespoon kosher salt, plus more as needed

Cracked black pepper

2 pounds bone-in, skin-on chicken legs, thighs, or drumsticks (4 legs or 8 thighs)

4 tablespoons grapeseed oil or other neutral oil, plus more for drizzling

1 bunch scallions (6 ounces)

½ pound shallots (5 or 6 large), halved or quartered

1½ pounds mixed root vegetables (such as yam, taro root, peeled cassava, carrot, or yellow beet), cut into 3- to 4-inch pieces

**for the dressing**

2 tablespoons sherry vinegar

1 tablespoon honey

1 tablespoon orange zest

¼ cup orange juice

¼ cup coconut milk

1 tablespoon red palm oil

Salt and black pepper

¼ cup fresh efirin (also known as scent leaf) or Thai basil leaves

¼ cup fresh cilantro leaves and tender stems

2 cups tender leafy greens, such as baby spinach or arugula

Preheat the oven to 450°F.

Coarsely crush the fennel seeds using the side of your knife or a mortar and pestle. Put the fennel seeds in a large bowl and add the salt and a few cracks of black pepper. Add the chicken and 2 tablespoons of the grapeseed oil and toss to coat.

Cut the scallions in two, separating the white and green parts, and set the green portions aside for the dressing. Place the scallion whites, shallots, and half of the root vegetables in a single layer on a sheet pan. Drizzle with the remaining 2 tablespoons grapeseed oil and season with salt and pepper. Arrange the chicken on top of the vegetables. Scatter the remaining root

vegetables around the chicken. Drizzle everything with more grapeseed oil. Roast until the chicken is golden and cooked through and the vegetables are tender and slightly crisped around the edges, 40 to 50 minutes.

Meanwhile, make the dressing: In a small bowl, combine the vinegar, honey, orange zest, orange juice, coconut milk, and red palm oil. Emulsify using a whisk or immersion blender. Slice the reserved scallion greens and stir them into the dressing. Season with salt and pepper.

Scatter the efirin and cilantro over the chicken and vegetables. Serve over leafy greens, with the citrusy dressing spooned over everything.

# spatchcock chicken
## with ginger, garlic, and green papaya

This dish is based on tinolang manok, a comforting Filipino chicken soup that Jenn de la Vega, author of *Showdown: Comfort Food, Chili & BBQ* and former *TASTE* Cook in Residence, grew up eating during sweater-weather season. She re-created the effect with this sheet pan dish, which includes healing moringa leaves, a bitter leafy green that helps shut down any oncoming cold (you can sub in arugula if you can't find moringa), and green papayas that take on the starchy role of potatoes. Green papaya is a great neutral-tasting firm fruit—you may have had it in a Thai green papaya salad, shredded and served with a citrusy dressing and chopped peanuts— but you can use winter squash or just chunks of potato instead of papaya and that will work really well, too. Just don't skimp on the pungent compound butter with fish sauce. Yes, you read that right. Get ready. **Serves 4 to 6**

1 (2-inch) piece fresh ginger, peeled and sliced

4 garlic cloves, peeled

4 tablespoons salted butter, at room temperature

2 tablespoons fish sauce

1 green papaya, peeled

1 red onion, quartered

1 (3- to 4-pound) whole chicken, patted dry

Salt and black pepper

¼ cup extra-virgin olive oil

2 cups moringa leaves or arugula

Preheat the oven to 425°F.

Mash the ginger and garlic together using a mortar and pestle or mince them finely to make a paste. In a small bowl, stir together the ginger-garlic paste, butter, and fish sauce. Set aside.

Slice the papaya in half lengthwise. Scoop out the seeds and pith with a spoon. Set the papaya halves cut-side down and slice them 1 inch thick. Separate the onion quarters into petals.

Remove the neck and gizzards from the chicken's cavity and discard (or save them for making stock or dog treats later). To spatchcock the chicken, place it breast-side down on a cutting board. Using kitchen scissors (if you have a cleaver or sharp chef's knife, you can use that—carefully— instead), snip along each side of the spine to remove it. Flip the chicken breast-side up, place your palm on the center of the breast, and push down until you feel the breastbone crack. This should help the chicken lie flat. Gently slide your finger underneath the skin of the breast to separate it from the meat a bit (this will encour-age the skin to crisp up in the oven). Rub the

butter–fish sauce mixture over the flesh of the chicken, underneath the skin. Tuck the wing tips underneath the wings to prevent them from burning. Sprinkle a generous amount of salt and pepper over the chicken and transfer it to a sheet pan, skin-side up. (At this point, if you have the time, you can refrigerate the chicken, uncovered, overnight in order to dry it out more, which will result in crispier skin.)

Arrange the papaya and onion in a single layer around the chicken. Drizzle the olive oil over everything. Roast the chicken for 10 minutes, then reduce the oven temperature to 400°F. Roast for another 20 minutes, then rotate the pan and flip the papaya pieces with tongs. Roast for another 20 minutes, or until a kitchen thermo-meter inserted into the thickest part of a thigh registers 160°F.

Remove the pan from the oven and let rest for 10 minutes. Sprinkle the moringa leaves over the pan to wilt. Carve the chicken and serve the pieces in a large serving bowl with the vegetables surrounding it and all the pan juices poured over.

# chicken-and-clam bake

A classic New England beach clam bake is one of those idyllic pastimes—like a whole pig roast—that are actually pretty difficult to pull off. Even if you have the opportunity to build a fire in a pit of sand on the beach and succeed in getting the rocks inside molten-hot to create ovenlike conditions, your home oven can do the trick just as well—without sand getting in your food. Who doesn't love a juicy mess of sweet corn, potatoes, and clams drenched in butter? Cue the sheet pan—it takes all of 10 minutes in the oven for littlenecks to go agape, spilling their brine across the pan to mix with melted butter and get absorbed by the potatoes. We're inviting chicken to this party, too—drumsticks or other handheld pieces with a classic Old Bay seasoning rub. All together, it's a finger-friendly, bib-worthy, nostalgic feast. **Serves 4**

1½ to 2 pounds bone-in, skin-on chicken parts

1 teaspoon Old Bay seasoning, plus more if needed

3 tablespoons extra-virgin olive oil

1½ pounds large red potatoes, quartered or cut into about 1-inch-wide wedges

2 ears corn, broken into thirds

Salt and black pepper

12 littleneck clams, scrubbed and soaked in cold water for 30 minutes

2 to 3 tablespoons butter, cut into small cubes

½ bunch parsley, chopped (optional)

Preheat the oven to 450°F.

Rub the chicken with the Old Bay and 1 tablespoon of the olive oil to coat thoroughly. Arrange the chicken on a sheet pan, leaving at least 1 inch between each piece. Toss the potatoes with 1 tablespoon of the olive oil in a large bowl and season with salt, pepper, and a couple shakes of Old Bay, if you like; toss again to coat. Arrange the potatoes on the pan with the chicken. Roast for 25 minutes.

Rub the corn pieces with the remaining 1 table-spoon olive oil. Rinse the clams under cold water and pat dry. Remove the sheet pan from the oven and carefully flip over each piece of chicken and all the potato pieces. Nestle the corn and the clams among the chicken and potatoes on the pan. Roast for 10 to 20 minutes, or until all the clams are fully open. (Discard any clams that have not opened after 20 minutes.)

Remove the pan from oven. Drop the butter cubes onto the pan and watch them melt. Using a metal fish spatula, loosen the chicken and potatoes from the pan and gently stir everything around to incorporate the melted butter into the juices from the clams and the chicken and coat the corn with this mixture.

Sprinkle the parsley over everything, if desired, and serve.

# roasted romaine chicken caesar

Heads up: Roasted romaine lettuce halves are nothing short of a revelation if you've only had your lettuce raw. Juicy and crisp, it's a little scandalous. This nod to chicken Caesar salad is warm, crunchy, and packed with all sorts of black pepperiness. I support making croutons out of big, torn chunks of bread, and that bread can be leftover and stale. But if you have a really nice loaf that's fresh and crusty on its own, skip the crouton-making steps here and just tear into it to mop up the juices in the pan. **Serves 4**

2 small heads romaine lettuce, trimmed of any wilted outer leaves and halved lengthwise

6 tablespoons extra-virgin olive oil

1 teaspoon salt, plus more as needed

Black peppercorns

2 whole boneless, skinless chicken breasts (1½ to 2 pounds total)

3 tablespoons whole black peppercorns

1 garlic clove, minced

½ rustic miche or any crusty peasant-style bread, torn into golf ball–size chunks or cubed

**for the dressing**

1 egg yolk

1 garlic clove, minced or grated

2 or 3 whole, oil-packed anchovies, minced (optional)

¼ teaspoon salt, plus more as needed

½ teaspoon Dijon mustard

½ cup extra-virgin olive oil

1 tablespoon fresh lemon juice, plus more as needed

¼ cup grated Parmigiano Reggiano cheese, plus more for serving

Rinse the romaine halves very well under running water, moving the leaves around to get the water in the nooks near the core. Shake them out and pat them completely dry with kitchen towels, or use a large salad spinner to help dry them out. The lettuce must be supremely dry, or else it won't crisp. (If you can get to it, try to do this a day or so ahead, whenever you first buy the lettuce.)

Preheat the oven to 450°F.

Smear the romaine halves with 1 tablespoon of the olive oil and sprinkle all over with a couple pinches each of salt and pepper. Place them cut-side down around the edge of a sheet pan.

Rub the chicken breasts with 1 tablespoon of the olive oil and sprinkle with ½ teaspoon of the salt. Place the peppercorns in a spice grinder and pulse only once or twice, briefly, to crack them. (Alternately, they can be crushed gently in a mortar and pestle.) Spread the cracked peppercorns on a flat plate. Press the top of each chicken breast into the cracked peppercorns a few times to coat its surface thoroughly. Arrange the chicken

in the center of the sheet pan, pepper-side up. Roast for 20 minutes.

Combine the remaining 4 tablespoons olive oil, the garlic, bread chunks, and a generous pinch each of salt and pepper in a bowl.

Remove the sheet pan from the oven and scatter the chunks of bread on top. Roast for 10 to 15 minutes, until a kitchen thermometer inserted into a breast registers 160°F.

Meanwhile, make the dressing: Whisk together the egg yolk, garlic, anchovies (if using), salt, and Dijon in a small bowl. While whisking continuously, very slowly drizzle in ¼ cup of the olive oil. Whisk in the lemon juice, then whisk in the remaining ¼ cup olive oil. Stir in the cheese. Taste for seasoning, adding more lemon juice or salt as needed.

Transfer the breasts to a cutting board and slice them along their length, across the grain, then return them to the pan (or transfer everything to a large serving platter or shallow bowl). Drizzle the dressing over everything, sprinkle with additional cheese, and serve.

# the best warm chicken salad
## with pan drippings vinaigrette

I love my cold chicken salad, but there's something so right about crispy, steaming chicken plopped atop a pile of well-dressed bitter greens. Roasting chicken will also lend drippings to spare, and hopefully some browned bits on the pan that will be excellent for mixing into a dressing shaped with Dijon mustard and red wine vinegar. And while we're roasting, some crisped winter squash can sub in for croutons to bulk up the salad. I've added fresh grapes and walnuts because we so often find those chunks bobbing about in cold, mayonnaise-bound chicken salads. They make great additions to a warm one, as do crumbles of pungent (in the best way) cheese like Gorgonzola. Feel free to mix up the fresh fruit, cheese, and nut options here to make *your* best warm chicken salad—or just the best one you can put together using what you have available (see photo on pages 58–59). **Serves 4 to 6**

2 bone-in, skin-on chicken breasts

3 to 4 tablespoons extra-virgin olive oil

2 teaspoons salt

1 teaspoon black pepper

1 delicata squash or other winter squash (except spaghetti squash), or 1 pound of cauliflower florets or sweet potatoes, cut into 1-inch-wide wedges

1 cup walnut halves or other nuts (optional)

2 tablespoons sherry vinegar or red wine vinegar

2 tablespoons finely chopped shallot

1 teaspoon Dijon mustard

1 small head radicchio or chicory, or 6 cups baby arugula

2 cups green grapes, halved

1 cup crumbled Gorgonzola or blue cheese

Preheat the oven to 450°F.

Rub the chicken breasts all over with 1 tablespoon of the olive oil and season with 1 teaspoon of the salt and ½ teaspoon of the pepper. Gently slide your finger underneath the skin of each breast to detach it from the meat a bit (this will encourage the skin to crisp up in the oven). Place the breasts on a sheet pan, skin-side up.

Slice the delicata squash crosswise into ½-inch-thick rings (to easily remove the seeds, scrape a butter knife around in the cavity once you have sliced a couple rings). If you're using a different winter squash, peel and cut it into small wedges about 1 inch thick. Put the squash in a large bowl and toss with about 1 tablespoon of the olive oil and a generous pinch each of salt

and pepper. Arrange the squash in a single layer around the chicken on the sheet pan so that no pieces are touching. Roast for 40 to 45 minutes, flipping the squash pieces after 20 minutes and adding the walnuts (if using) to the pan for the last 5 minutes of roasting.

Remove the squash and walnuts from the sheet pan and set aside. Let the chicken pieces cool on the pan for a couple of minutes, then carefully remove the rib cage and any other bones and discard them. Transfer the meat to a cutting board, reserving any juices that have found their way onto the pan, and slice the breasts across the grain into roughly 1-inch-thick slices.

Pour the vinegar onto the sheet pan where the chicken had been. Scrape up any golden brown bits from the pan, then scrape the vinegar and any chicken juices and drippings on the pan into a small bowl; add any juices or bits from the cutting board as well. Add the shallot and mustard and whisk to combine. Whisk in the remaining 1 to 2 tablespoons of olive oil. Taste and adjust the seasoning with more salt, pepper, vinegar, or oil.

Tear the radicchio leaves into bite-size pieces and put them in a large bowl. Add half the dressing and toss to coat. Arrange the dressed radicchio on individual serving plates (or on a large platter for serving family-style) and top with the roasted squash, chicken breast slices, grapes, walnuts, and Gorgonzola. Drizzle with the remaining dressing and serve.

# chicken and eggplant
## with spiced tomatoes

Shakshuka—the wildly popular Middle Eastern skillet of eggs poached in spiced tomatoes and red pepper—does not work very faithfully on a sheet pan, but I couldn't resist this adaptation. Roasting the vegetables instead will give them some char to deepen their flavors, and instead of eggs, we can add other ingredients that roast nicely, like egg*plant*, and, well, the source of all eggs: chicken. I love the custardy meat of roasted eggplant halves and how easy it is to create a tomatoey spiced stew by filling the sheet pan to the edges with fresh tomatoes, onions, and peppers. The Arabic word *shakshuka* does, after all, mean "a haphazard mixture" or "all mixed up"—not "a mixture that must have eggs." I've tried this out with big chunks of zucchini and summer squash instead of eggplant, and that was a great mix, too. Serve this with some warm pita or crusty bread on the side to sop up the coriander-and-cumin-spiked gravy. **Serves 4 to 6**

1 medium eggplant (about ½ pound)

2½ teaspoons salt, plus more as needed

8 plum tomatoes, coarsely chopped

1 red onion, chopped

1 large red bell pepper, chopped

2 garlic cloves, minced

2 teaspoons ground cumin

2 teaspoons ground coriander

1 teaspoon paprika

1 teaspoon black pepper

½ teaspoon cayenne pepper

6 tablespoons extra-virgin olive oil

2 pounds bone-in, skin-on chicken legs, thighs, or drumsticks

Crispy Kale Crown (page 29; optional)

4 ounces feta cheese, crumbled

½ cup fresh cilantro leaves and tender stems or flat-leaf parsley, chopped

Halve the eggplant lengthwise. Using the tip of a knife, make three or four vertical slashes into the flesh of each half, but be carefully not to cut through to the skin. Sprinkle the cut sides of the eggplant with generous pinches of salt to coat thoroughly. Set aside on a plate for 20 minutes.

Preheat the oven to 450°F.

Combine the tomatoes, onion, bell pepper, half of the garlic, 1 teaspoon of the salt, 1 teaspoon of the cumin, 1 teaspoon of the coriander, ½ teaspoon of the paprika, ½ teaspoon of the black pepper, ¼ teaspoon of the cayenne, and 2 tablespoons of the olive oil on a sheet pan and toss to incorporate thoroughly.

Squeeze each eggplant half gently and shake off any drops of liquid that have come to the surface. Wipe the cut sides with a paper towel. Smear each half with a tablespoon or so of olive oil and place them on the sheet pan, cut-side down, surrounded by the other vegetables, making sure they both have full contact with the pan. Using the tip of a knife, prick the skin of the eggplant a few times.

Rub the chicken with 1 tablespoon of the olive oil, ½ teaspoon of the salt, the remaining 1 teaspoon cumin, 1 teaspoon coriander, ½ teaspoon paprika, ½ teaspoon black pepper, and ¼ teaspoon cayenne. Arrange the chicken on the sheet pan, nestled in among the vegetables (the tomato mixture does not have to stay in an even layer).

Roast for 25 minutes, then toss the tomato mixture around on the pan (do not flip the eggplant halves) and rotate the pan. If adding a Crispy Kale Crown, see instructions on page 29 and add it now. Roast for 10 to 15 minutes more, or until the eggplant feels very soft to the touch, the chicken is browned, and a kitchen thermometer inserted into the thickest part of a thigh registers 160°F.

Flip the eggplant halves over on the pan with a spatula and cut them into a few sections each, removing the tip with the stem. Scatter the feta over everything, garnish with the cilantro, and serve.

# chicken satay lettuce wraps
## with peanut sauce and quick pickles

Satay, chunks of marinated meat grilled on a stick and oftentimes dipped into piquant sauces, has been around much longer than the Asian fusion restaurants that have famously served them since the 1990s. It originated in Indonesia, having evolved from the kebabs eaten by Middle Eastern traders making their way on the spice route to the Far East. Since satay has been adopted throughout Southeast Asia, there are endless varieties of marinades for the meat and sauces to serve with the skewers, but the iconic Indonesian-style preparation includes a sweet-and-spicy peanut dipping sauce and refreshing pickles on the side. And in some wonderful breaking news, not all satays need to be marinated overnight; a hefty rub of dry spices before placing the chicken underneath a broiler makes for a tasty protein that's ready to serve in no time (okay, 10 to 15 minutes). The lettuce cups are optional, but they make a great vessel for you to pile your chunk of chicken, dollop of sauce, and pinch of pickles into before crushing it. For a starch, try serving it with flatbread, sesame noodles (page 113), sticky rice (page 118), ham fried rice (page 112), or just plain steamed rice. **Serves 4**

1 teaspoon coriander seeds

½ teaspoon cumin seeds

1½ pounds boneless, skinless chicken thighs or breasts, cut into 1-inch cubes

1 small garlic clove, grated

1 tablespoon soy sauce

1 teaspoon sugar

½ teaspoon salt

½ teaspoon ground turmeric

2 tablespoons vegetable oil or coconut oil

**for the peanut sauce**

¼ cup finely chopped onion or shallots

1 garlic clove, minced

¼ cup peanut butter

¼ cup water

1 tablespoon fresh lime juice

1 teaspoon fish sauce

1 tablespoon sambal oelek (Indonesian chile paste) or sriracha (optional)

1 tablespoon sugar

¼ teaspoon salt

¼ cup roasted peanuts, chopped (optional)

1 small head Bibb, Boston, or Little Gem lettuce, or ½ head iceberg lettuce, leaves separated

1 recipe Quick-Pickled Carrot, Onion, and Radishes (page 127)

¼ cup fresh cilantro leaves (optional)

Preheat the broiler.

Toast the coriander and cumin seeds in a small dry pan over high heat, shaking frequently, for 1 to 2 minutes, until fragrant. Immediately transfer them to a spice grinder and pulse for a few seconds, until the spices are well ground.

Combine the chicken, ground coriander and cumin, garlic, soy sauce, sugar, salt, turmeric, and vegetable oil in a large bowl and mix thoroughly. Thread the chicken onto four bamboo or metal skewers and place them in a single layer on a

sheet pan. Broil for about 5 minutes, until the edges are crisp and browning, then carefully flip the skewers using tongs and broil for another 5 minutes, until browned and crispy.

Meanwhile, make the sauce: Combine the onion, garlic, peanut butter, water, lime juice, fish sauce, sambal, sugar, salt, and peanuts (if using) in a medium bowl and mix well.

Serve the satay skewers with the lettuce, pickles, cilantro (if using) and peanut sauce on the side, so diners can make their own wraps.

# dak dori sheet pan chicken

The spicy and hearty Korean chicken soup dak dori tang (or dak bokkeum tang) is a cool-weather balm of chicken stewed with chunks of potatoes and carrots. As a homestyle dish, it may vary in terms of the vegetable additions, but its intense and flavorful broth is uniform: a deep, cloudy maroon, laced with gochugaru (Korean red chile flakes) and gochujang, a pungent and spicy fermented soybean and chile paste. I had my first bowl of it many years ago at Han Bat, one of my favorite restaurants in New York City's Koreatown, and knew I had to learn to make it. For this dish, we're skipping the broth to focus more on the chicken part, which gets its own maroon glaze toward the end of cooking. I wouldn't try to substitute another type of chile flake for the gochugaru, because it has such a distinct, smoky-sweet flavor and is seedless, so a little goes a long way, heat-wise. It can be ordered online easily and is stocked in many large supermarkets nowadays. **Serves 3 or 4**

1½ to 2 pounds bone-in, skin-on chicken legs, thighs, whole wings, or party wings (see Note)

1 garlic clove, grated

1 tablespoon toasted sesame oil

1 teaspoon salt

1 teaspoon white pepper

1 teaspoon gochugaru (Korean chile flakes)

1 pound fingerling potatoes, halved lengthwise into uniform pieces no thicker than 1 inch

½ pound carrots, halved lengthwise and cut into 2-inch-long segments (no thicker than 1 inch)

3 tablespoons neutral oil, such as grapeseed

½ cup beech mushrooms

**for the sauce**

1 tablespoon minced fresh ginger

1 tablespoon minced garlic

1 tablespoon soy sauce

1 tablespoon sugar

¼ cup mirin

2 tablespoons gochujang (Korean chile paste)

2 teaspoons fish sauce

1 tablespoon water

¼ teaspoon white pepper

2 tablespoons toasted sesame seeds

2 scallions, thinly sliced

**NOTE** If using party wings, roast for the first 20 minutes as specified, toss, and glaze (do not roast the additional 10 minutes before glazing). Roast for 10 to 15 minutes after glazing.

Preheat the oven to 425°F.

Combine the chicken, garlic, sesame oil, ½ teaspoon of the salt, ½ teaspoon of the white pepper, and ½ teaspoon of the gochugaru in a large bowl and toss to coat. Arrange the chicken on a sheet pan. Toss the potatoes, carrots, 2 tablespoons of the neutral oil, and the remaining ½ teaspoon salt, ½ teaspoon white pepper, and ½ teaspoon gochugaru in a large bowl. Spread the vegetables on the sheet pan in a single layer around and between the chicken. Roast for 20 minutes.

In a bowl, separate the beech mushrooms from their stem into smaller clumps of a uniform size (about ½ inch thick). Toss them with the remaining 1 tablespoon neutral oil.

Meanwhile, make the sauce: In a small bowl, stir together the ginger, garlic, soy sauce, sugar, mirin, gochujang, fish sauce, water, and white pepper.

After 20 minutes of roasting, toss or flip the vegetables and chicken, scatter the mushrooms all over, and rotate the pan. Roast for another 10 minutes, then remove the pan from the oven. Give the chicken and vegetables a toss as you drizzle the sauce over everything. Roast for another 10 to 15 minutes.

Scatter the sesame seeds and scallions over everything and serve.

# pimentón chicken
## with shishito peppers and patatas bravas

Bar food doesn't get much respect in the United States (although I'll never say no to a pile of loaded nachos or tater tots). But in Spain, bar food bites, known as tapas, are a major highlight on a night out of drinking. One of those quintessential tapas is patatas bravas, fried potatoes with a tomatoey paprika sauce and mayonnaise. Inspiration called, and here we're crisping up some potato wedges alongside chicken, some dry-cured chorizo slices, and whole shishito peppers for a ridiculously good sheet pan version. For the patatas bravas sauce, tomatoes and onions are roasted, then blended with oil and vinegar. The imperative spice here is pimentón, a Spanish paprika with a haunting smokiness. Pimentón de la Vera, from the La Vera region in Spain, is the kind you're looking for to get this superlative flavor; traditionally, the peppers were dried in a barn with a fire burning nearby to help speed the process in the region's damp, cool climate. **Serves 4**

2 pounds bone-in, skin-on chicken parts (thighs, legs, drumsticks, breasts, or whole wings)

1½ pounds small waxy potatoes, such as red or Yukon Gold, quartered

2 teaspoons sweet or hot pimentón, plus more as needed

2 garlic cloves, grated

1½ teaspoons salt, plus more if needed

4 tablespoons extra-virgin olive oil, plus more if needed

1 cup halved grape tomatoes

1 red onion, quartered

8 to 10 shishito or baby bell peppers, whole

2 to 4 ounces hard, dry-cured Spanish chorizo, sliced into ½-inch-thick rounds (about ½ cup)

1 tablespoon red wine vinegar

¼ cup water (optional)

Black pepper (optional)

Crispy Kale Crown (page 29; optional)

**NOTE** You can skip making the sauce and just serve the roasted tomatoes and onions with the rest of your dish, if desired.

Preheat the oven to 450°F.

Combine the chicken, potatoes, pimentón, garlic, 1 teaspoon of the salt, and 2 tablespoons of the olive oil in a large bowl and mix well. Spread the chicken and potatoes over half of a sheet pan, being sure to place the potatoes cut-side down in a single layer. Combine the tomatoes, onion, ¼ teaspoon of the salt, and 1 tablespoon of the olive oil in a medium bowl and toss to coat, allowing the onions to separate into smaller chunks. Arrange the tomatoes and onion on the other half of the sheet pan. Roast for 20 minutes.

Meanwhile, rub the shishito peppers with the remaining 1 tablespoon olive oil and season with the remaining ¼ teaspoon salt.

After 20 minutes of roasting, remove the sheet pan from the oven. Scrape the tomatoes and onions off the pan into a bowl and put the shishito peppers

on the pan in their place. Nestle the chorizo slices in between everything on the sheet pan. Roast for another 5 to 10 minutes, until the chicken is well browned on top and a kitchen thermometer inserted into the thickest part of a thigh close to the bone registers 160°F.

Meanwhile, if desired, transfer the roasted tomatoes and onions to a food processor or blender. Add the vinegar and process until smooth, stopping to scrape down the sides as needed. If necessary, add extra olive oil, water, or vinegar to help blend. Taste the sauce and season with salt and pepper or pimentón.

Drizzle the sauce over the potatoes and dust them with pimentón, then serve.

# blackened chicken
## with andouille sausage, okra, and tomatoes

The heady spices in Cajun seasoning blends—ground chiles, garlic, and often celery salt—take on more dimension when cooked to a crisp on a piece of chicken or fish. The term "blackened" is associated with skillet cooking and was popularized by the New Orleans chef Paul Prudhomme, who wrote eleven cookbooks in the 1980s and '90s and sold a lot of seasoning blends. Blackening entailed coating a filet all over with seasoning before searing it on a skillet to blacken the surface. But as an easy alternative, we're taking the concept of copious seasoning and broiling the chicken to acquire some char. I am very much pro-okra, slimy guts and all, but when okra pods are cut up and roasted or broiled, you'll notice that the slime virtually disappears. (If you're still a little wary of it, go ahead and replace the okra with another vegetable, like some broccoli florets.) Finally, I've added some andouille sausage, a pork sausage that originated in France but is perhaps nowhere more loved than in Louisiana. **Serves 4**

1½ to 2 pounds boneless, skinless chicken breasts or thighs

2 teaspoons paprika

1 teaspoon onion powder

1 teaspoon garlic powder, or 1 garlic clove, grated

½ to 1 teaspoon cayenne pepper (depending on how spicy you like it)

½ teaspoon black pepper

½ teaspoon celery salt (optional)

1 teaspoon salt (or 1½ teaspoons if not using celery salt)

3 tablespoons extra-virgin olive oil

1 andouille sausage link, cut into ½ to 1-inch chunks

½ pound fresh whole okra pods, sliced into ¼- to ½-inch rounds

1 pint cherry or grape tomatoes, halved

Preheat the broiler.

Rub the chicken with the paprika, onion powder, garlic powder, cayenne, black pepper, celery salt (if using), salt, and 2 tablespoons of the olive oil. Arrange the chicken on a sheet pan. Combine the sausage, okra, and tomatoes in a large bowl and toss with the remaining 1 tablespoon olive oil. Scatter the sausage and vegetables between and around the chicken on the pan. Broil for 10 minutes. Flip the sausage and vegetables and rotate the pan. Broil for another 10 to 15 minutes, or until the chicken is cooked through (this may vary depending on the size of the boneless breasts or thighs used). To serve, transfer the chicken to a platter and spread the vegetables and sausage around. Scrape any juices from the pan and pour over the chicken.

# za'atar-rubbed chicken
## with carrots, beets, and labne

Za'atar, a dried herb blend commonly used throughout the Middle East, is a responsible way to get high. I first started cooking with it after a friend gave me a little plastic baggie of the stuff from her trip to Jerusalem, and its spruce-y, tangy, nutty flavors got me lost in a storm of flatbread baking for much of that month. This blend is variable (see the spice chart on page 21), but it usually has a base of dried thyme or sometimes oregano, sesame seeds, and ground sumac, which gives it a smack of sourness. It's great rubbed on chicken before roasting—use it for a whole chicken, like Weeknight Spatchcock Chicken with Lemon and Root Vegetables (page 24), instead of herbes de Provence sometime. Here the roasted spice blend infuses the oils of the chicken and some humble root vegetables, waking them up a bit. For a creamy, tangy finish, this dish is served atop luscious smears of labne, a strained yogurt that's even thicker than Greek yogurt and often mistaken for a cheese. **Serves 4**

1½ to 2 pounds bone-in, skin-on chicken legs or thighs

1 pound carrots (can be a mixture of colors), halved lengthwise (and quartered, if thicker than 1 inch)

1 pound beets (can be a mix of types, such as Chioggia or golden), quartered or cut into eighths, to make wedges about 1 inch thick

1 medium red onion, quartered

¼ cup extra-virgin olive oil

3 tablespoons za'atar (store-bought, or you can make your own based on the ingredients found in the chart on page 21, using about 2 tablespoons of dried thyme, oregano and/or marjoram, and a tablespoon of the other spices combined)

1 teaspoon salt

½ teaspoon black pepper

¼ cup pine nuts (optional)

About 4 ounces labne or Greek yogurt

½ cup fresh parsley or mint (optional)

Preheat the oven to 450°F.

Spread the chicken, carrots, beets, and onion over a sheet pan. Drizzle with the olive oil and season with the za'atar, salt, and pepper. Place the chicken skin-side up and the carrots and beets cut-side down. Roast for 20 minutes, then flip the carrots and beets and rotate the pan. Roast for another 15 to 20 minutes, until the chicken skin is very crisp and a kitchen thermometer inserted into the thickest part of a thigh registers 160°F.

Meanwhile, toast the pine nuts (if using) in a small saucepan over medium-high heat just until they brown lightly, 2 to 3 minutes. Remove from the heat and set aside.

Spread the labne all over the bottom of a large serving dish. Place the roasted chicken and vegetables on top. Scatter the toasted pine nuts and the parsley (if using) over everything and serve.

# tomatillo chicken
## with potatoes, poblanos, and sweet corn

One of my favorite breakfast dishes is chilaquiles verdes, a Mexican dish of tortilla chips with scraps of meat that's smothered with green sauce and melted cheese. *Chilaquiles* comes from the Nahuatl word for "chiles and greens"–and although you can get it served with a red sauce, I love how a green salsa, with a base of tart tomatillos, really helps wake me up. Tomatillo salsa is simple to make, and before blending it up, you can roast the tomatillos in the same sheet pan as–you guessed it–some chicken. Meanwhile, a breakfast-worthy hash of potatoes, poblanos, and sweet corn sizzle on the same pan. That's a riff on patatas y poblanos, a popular taco filling that sounds humble but tastes much better than the sum of its parts. **Serves 3 or 4**

1 pound tomatillos, husked, and halved from top to bottom

1 small yellow onion or shallot, halved

2 garlic cloves, smashed, plus 1 garlic clove, grated, or 1 teaspoon garlic powder

1 jalapeño, stemmed, halved lengthwise, and seeded

4 tablespoons extra-virgin olive oil

¾ teaspoon salt, plus more as needed

1 pound potatoes, cut into ½-inch cubes

2 poblano peppers, stemmed, seeded, and finely diced

¼ teaspoon black pepper

1½ to 2 pounds bone-in, skin-on chicken thighs or legs, or boneless, skinless thighs

½ teaspoon ground cumin

½ teaspoon paprika

¼ teaspoon cayenne pepper

Kernels from 2 ears sweet corn

½ cup cilantro leaves and tender greens, chopped

About 4 ounces queso fresco or cotija cheese, crumbled

2 scallions, chopped

Preheat the oven to 450°F.

Combine the tomatillos, onion, smashed garlic cloves, jalapeño, 1 tablespoon of the olive oil, and ¼ teaspoon of the salt on a sheet pan and toss to coat. Arrange the tomatillos cut-side up on one half of a sheet pan. Scatter the onion, garlic, and jalapeño between and around the tomatillos.

Combine the potatoes, poblanos, 2 tablespoons of the olive oil, ½ teaspoon of the salt, and the black pepper in a large bowl and toss to coat. Scatter the potatoes and poblanos over the other half of the pan.

Toss the chicken pieces with the grated garlic, cumin, paprika, cayenne, and the remaining 1 tablespoon olive oil. Arrange the chicken skin-side up on the sheet pan, nestled among the vegetables. (If you're using boneless thighs, hold off on adding them to the pan.) Roast for 20 minutes.

Remove the sheet pan from the oven and transfer the roasted tomatillos, onion, garlic cloves, and jalapeño to a blender. Add the corn kernels to the pan and toss them around with the potatoes and poblanos. Roast for 5 to 10 minutes longer if using boneless thighs, or 10 to 15 minutes if using bone-in thighs, until the chicken is cooked through.

Meanwhile, add ¼ cup of the cilantro to the blender with the tomatillo mixture and blend until smooth. Taste the sauce and season with salt.

Drizzle the tomatillo sauce over the chicken and vegetables. Scatter the crumbled queso all over, garnish with the scallions and remaining cilantro, and serve.

# vietnamese-style stuffed tomatoes
## with wilted spinach and leeks

Eye-catching but not too twee, and much more filling than stuffed mushroom hors d'oeuvres, these stuffed tomato halves are like juicy purses overflowing with ground chicken. I learned about Vietnamese pan-fried stuffed tomatoes from Andrea Nguyen's cookbook *Vietnamese Food Any Day,* in which she explained that they were created by inventive Vietnamese cooks who hybridized popular French foods. They're made with ground pork seasoned with fish sauce and onion, but I was delighted to find that with the help of a little extra chicken or duck fat, a chicken version was just as tasty. I've made them with some crispy spirals of roasted leek slices and some fresh spinach that gently wilts for the last few minutes of roasting; alternatively, you could do a Crispy Kale Crown (page 29). **Serves 4**

4 tablespoons neutral oil, such as grapeseed

1 pound ground chicken

2 tablespoons rendered chicken or duck fat (optional)

4 scallions, chopped, or ⅓ cup finely chopped onion

½ cup cooked rice

1 tablespoon fish sauce

1 teaspoon sugar

½ teaspoon salt

¼ teaspoon black pepper

4 firm medium tomatoes on the vine

1 fat leek, white and light green parts only, rinsed well and sliced into ½-inch-thick rounds

1 bunch fresh spinach

Preheat the oven to 400°F. Lightly grease a sheet pan with 2 tablespoons of the neutral oil, to ensure the tomatoes don't stick.

Combine the ground chicken, rendered fat (if using), scallions, cooked rice, fish sauce, sugar, ¼ teaspoon of the salt, and the pepper in a large bowl and gently mix with your hands (don't over-mix, or the chicken mixture will become tough).

Halve the tomatoes from top to bottom. Using a sharp-edged spoon, such as a tablespoon measure or a melon baller, gently scoop out the tomato seeds and pulp and discard (or reserve for another use). Divide the chicken mixture into 8 equal portions, roll each into a ball, and place one ball in each tomato half. Gently pat down the top of the ball to create a flattened surface.

Place the tomato halves on the sheet pan filling-side up, leaving a couple of inches between each. Place the sliced leek rounds around and between the tomatoes. Roast for 20 minutes.

Meanwhile, toss the spinach with the remaining 2 tablespoons neutral oil and ¼ teaspoon salt. Remove the crisped leek rounds from the pan and set aside on a plate. Scatter the seasoned spinach leaves between and around the tomatoes. Roast for another 10 to 15 minutes, until the tomatoes are soft and the spinach is wilted and a little crisp at the edges.

Serve the stuffed tomatoes with the crisped leeks and spinach on the side.

# mustard chicken
## with bacon, mushrooms, and onions

This dish, which I'll call an homage, brings to mind some of my favorite French-food tropes: there's a lot of onions, heavy cream, and bacon, and yet it's somehow balanced and refined-tasting, thanks to the inclusion of mustard, in this case. Some dishes that came to mind when I was making it include coq au Riesling (the sort of white wine sister to boeuf Bourguignon), tarte flambée (an Alsatian bacon, onion, and cream pie), and, of course, poulet à la moutarde—that's mustard chicken, a homey stew thickened with Dijon and cream. Carrots and celery root would be a nice addition if you can fit those pieces in the pan, but for me, I want plenty of potatoes to soak up this rich and robust sauce. I also love using a whole-grain type of mustard sometimes called moutarde à l'ancienne, or "old world–style," for a little texture on the chicken, but it's perfectly fine to use a Dijon here throughout. Make it on a cold winter night and pick out an old French movie starring Catherine Deneuve, like *The Umbrellas of Cherbourg*, to watch while you eat it. **Serves 4**

2 pounds bone-in, skin-on chicken pieces (legs, thighs, drumsticks, or breasts)

1½ pounds potatoes, preferably a waxy variety such as red or Yukon Gold, quartered or cut into roughly 2-inch-wide wedges

1 garlic clove, grated

1 tablespoon whole-grain mustard (or additional Dijon)

4 tablespoons extra-virgin olive oil

1 teaspoon salt, plus more as needed

½ teaspoon black pepper, plus more as needed

2 yellow onions, thinly sliced

8 to 10 ounces button mushrooms, sliced

2 or 3 thick-cut bacon slices, cut crosswise into ½-inch-wide pieces

2 tablespoons Dijon mustard

1 cup heavy cream

2 teaspoons fresh thyme leaves, plus 6 to 8 thyme sprigs, and additional leaves for garnish

Preheat the oven to 425°F.

Combine the chicken, potatoes, garlic, whole-grain mustard, 2 tablespoons of the olive oil, ½ teaspoon of the salt, and ¼ teaspoon of the black pepper in a large bowl and toss to coat. Arrange the chicken and potatoes on a sheet pan in a single layer.

Combine the onions, mushrooms, bacon, and the remaining 2 tablespoons olive oil, ½ teaspoon salt, and ¼ teaspoon black pepper in a large bowl and toss to coat. Spread the onions and mushrooms between and around the chicken pieces (these can be piled up—no need to arrange them in an even layer). Roast for 30 minutes, rotating the pan halfway through the cooking time.

Meanwhile, in a small bowl, stir together the Dijon, cream, thyme leaves, and a pinch each of salt and pepper.

After 30 minutes of roasting, remove the pan from the oven and toss the onions and mushrooms to release any pieces that are sticking to the pan. Smother each chicken piece with the cream mixture, and drizzle the excess cream mixture across the whole sheet pan to use it up. Place the thyme sprigs around the pan. Roast for another 20 minutes, until the chicken is golden brown and its internal temperature reaches 160°F with a thermometer inserted into the thickest part of a piece.

Sprinkle additional thyme leaves over the top and serve.

# 2

# worth the wait

The difference between only-okay roast chicken and sublime roast chicken is not always easy to pinpoint. But it's often the case that the chicken got a boost from resting in a flavor-packed marinade for a while (perhaps overnight), or from curing in a salt rub for a few hours to draw out moisture, so that when the chicken met a full blast of dry heat, its skin turned brittle like toffee. Some of my favorite chicken dishes just can't happen without an overnight step like this.

For instance, it won't do much to rub some soy sauce on chicken right before roasting it; it really needs to get under the chicken's skin (in all seriousness!), staining the thighs and breasts a warm reddish hue—and deeply seasoning it in the process. This only happens over several hours. Many of the recipes in this section call for an overnight marinade, but it's a bit more flexible than that. Sometimes, two hours is all the time you have, and that's fine. Sometimes, your dinner plans change and you end up marinating a chicken for two or three days. I've been there many times, sometimes freezing marinated chicken that had to be postponed until a far later date. Consider it planning way ahead. Consider waiting. It's almost always (or strictly always, in the case of this collection of recipes) worth it.

# dry-brined whole chicken
## with fennel and cipollini onions

I love opening the fridge and seeing a whole chicken drying out. It reminds me of the scene in the indie '80s film *Withnail and I* where the two protagonists go to the countryside and have to figure out what to eat; they place a chicken sitting upright in the oven, an image that makes me crack up every time. I don't recommend you force a chicken to sit up straight while it's roasting, but I kind of do if you're dry-brining it overnight. If you can get your chicken to sit up, that gives most of its skin exposure to air, which is the point of dry-brining it. That and gently curing the bird with salt and pepper helps leach some of the moisture out of its skin, paving the way to the crispiest golden skin. I love the refreshingly sweet, slow-roasted fennel and onions with a delicate white wine jus in this recipe. But if you don't like the combination, simply replace it with chunks of any firm vegetables, like in Weeknight Spatchcock Chicken (page 24). **Serves 4 to 6**

1 (3½- to 4-pound) whole chicken

1 tablespoon plus ½ teaspoon salt

1¼ teaspoons black pepper, plus more as needed

1 large fennel bulb

8 to 10 small cipollini onions

2 to 3 tablespoons extra-virgin olive oil

12 to 15 fresh sage leaves, very thinly sliced, or 2 to 3 tablespoons fresh thyme leaves

4 tablespoons unsalted butter, at room temperature

½ cup dry white wine

1 lemon, halved (optional)

Remove the neck and gizzards from the chicken's cavity and discard (or save them for making stock or dog treats later). Season the chicken all over its surface and inside the cavity with 1 tablespoon of the salt and 1 teaspoon of the pepper. Place the bird in a casserole dish or another shallow dish large enough that the chicken does not touch the sides of the dish, and refrigerate, uncovered, for 12 to 24 hours. (To allow both sides a chance to dry equally, place it breast-side down to start, then flip it over halfway through so it's breast-side up for its remaining time in the fridge. If you don't think you'll be able to get to it or fear you'll forget to flip it, then try to stand the chicken upright in the dish or just place it on its back from the start so that the breast is exposed to the air.)

Preheat the oven to 450°F.

Cut the stalks and fronds from the fennel bulb and set aside. Quarter the fennel bulb through the root end and, if the quarters are large, halve each one so the pieces are no wider than about

2 inches. Pick the fronds from the stalks and reserve the freshest-looking ones for garnish. Cut the stalks into 1-inch sections (discard any dry or tough-looking parts toward the top).

Put the fennel bulb and stalks on a sheet pan and add the onions, olive oil, half of the sage, and the remaining ½ teaspoon salt and ¼ teaspoon pepper. Toss to combine. Arrange the vegetables in a single layer, leaving some room in the center for the chicken.

Combine the butter and the remaining sage in a small bowl.

Pat the chicken dry with paper towels. To spatchcock the chicken, place it breast-side down on a cutting board. Using kitchen scissors (if you have a cleaver or sharp chef's knife, you can use that—carefully—instead), snip along each side of the spine to remove it. Flip the chicken breast-side up, place your palm on the center of the breast, and push down until you feel the breastbone crack. This should help the chicken lie flat.

Gently slide your finger underneath the skin of the breast to detach it from the meat a bit (this will encourage the skin to crisp up in the oven).

Place the chicken in the center of the sheet pan, moving the vegetables so they're evenly spaced around the chicken. Rub the sage butter all over the chicken and carefully slide some butter underneath the chicken's skin, especially over the breast (be careful not to tear the skin). Sprinkle the top of the bird with a bit more pepper.

Roast for 20 minutes, then reduce the oven temperature to 350°F and roast for another 20 minutes. Pour the wine all over the vegetables and roast for another 20 minutes, or until the chicken's skin is very crisp and a kitchen thermometer inserted into the thickest part of a thigh registers 160°F. Remove the pan from the oven and let the chicken sit for a few minutes.

Carve the chicken and arrange it on a platter with the vegetables. Pour all the juices from the sheet pan over the top. Garnish with some of the reserved fennel fronds, arrange the lemon halves on the side (if using), and serve.

# coconut adobo chicken
## with crispy radish and bok choy

Bright with acidity and loaded with garlic and ginger, the classic Filipino coconut chicken adobo is one of those dishes that's too good not to reinterpret on a sheet pan. There are a lot of ways to make this (typically long-simmered) stew of chicken with coconut milk, vinegar, soy sauce, and bay leaves, and some prefer a less soupy braise. I make mine the way I was taught by a Filipino cook I once worked beside in a now-shuttered ramen bar. The ingredients are surprisingly few in number but surprisingly plentiful in amount, and you had to (HAD to!) start making the adobo the night before by submerging your chicken in it; otherwise, the chicken wouldn't be as intensely flavored, and it wouldn't really be adobo. I took that wisdom to the land of chicken wings for this recipe, although you could use any bone-in chicken piece and bump up the roasting time. It's one of the recipes that can sit around in its marinade another day, so if pizza comes calling the night you had intended to make it, no worries. It will prob be better on night two. **Serves 4**

1 cup soy sauce

1 cup rice vinegar (preferably Chinese black vinegar)

½ cup packed brown sugar

8 garlic cloves, smashed

1 (2-inch) piece fresh ginger, peeled and chopped

4 bay leaves

1 teaspoon salt

2 pounds bone-in chicken thighs, drumsticks, whole wings, or party wings

2 tablespoons coconut oil

8 small radishes, halved

2 small heads baby bok choy, halved

1 (14-ounce) can full-fat coconut milk

2 scallions, thinly sliced

Combine the soy sauce, vinegar, brown sugar, garlic, ginger, bay leaves, and salt in a large airtight container or zip-top bag. Stir well to dissolve the sugar and salt. Add the chicken and submerge them in the marinade. Cover the container or seal the bag and marinate in the refrigerator for at least 24 hours or up to 48 hours.

Preheat the oven to 450°F. Grease a sheet pan with the coconut oil.

Remove the chicken from the container or bag, shaking off any excess marinade, and arrange them skin-side down on the prepared sheet pan, making sure no pieces are touching (reserve the marinade). Arrange the radish halves and bok choy cut-side down in a single layer around the chicken. Roast for 20 minutes.

Meanwhile, pour the marinade into a small saucepan and add the coconut milk. Bring to a boil over medium-high heat, then reduce to a simmer and cook, stirring occasionally, until the sauce has reduced to about 1 cup.

After 20 minutes in the oven, carefully flip the chicken and toss the vegetables around. Roast for another 10 minutes, or until the chicken skin is very crisp and the vegetables are evenly browned. If using bone-in thighs or drumsticks, roast until a kitchen thermometer inserted near the thickest part of one piece reaches 160°F. Transfer the chicken to a large bowl and toss with the sauce.

Serve the chicken and roasted vegetables on a platter, garnished with the scallions.

# cornell sauce sheet pan chicken
## with summer veggie sizzle

If my family grilled chicken when I was growing up, it was either Mom's Soy Sauce Chicken (page 93) or chicken with Cornell sauce. My paternal grandparents spoke of Cornell sauce chicken as if it were as common as hamburgers or hot dogs. They lived in Elmira, New York, which is located fairly close to Cornell University, my dad and brother's alma mater and the birthplace of this barbecue sauce recipe—a vinegary, herbal sauce made a shocking shade of *white* thanks to an egg used to emulsify the oil. It's similar to Alabama-style white barbecue sauce, but it's used to both marinate the chicken as well as baste it later when it's on the grill. Skipping the basting part and moving it to a sheet pan, the chicken is still fragrant and juicy thanks to all that marinade. And you can add a few summer vegetables—which remind me of my grandfather's vegetable patch upstate—in between the chicken pieces to absorb some of the juices. **Serves 4 to 6**

**for the marinade**

1 egg

1 cup vegetable oil

2 cups apple cider vinegar

2 tablespoons salt

1 teaspoon black pepper

1 tablespoon poultry seasoning (store-bought, or see the spice chart on page 21 to make your own)

1 (3- to 4-pound) whole chicken, halved, quartered, or spatchcocked (see page 24), or use bone-in, skin-on pieces of all the same kind

1 pound red potatoes, diced

1 large zucchini, diced

1 pint grape tomatoes, halved

3 tablespoons extra-virgin olive oil

½ teaspoon salt

¼ teaspoon black pepper

1 cup corn kernels (cut from 2 ears fresh sweet corn)

½ cup fresh basil leaves, torn (optional)

Make the marinade: Beat the egg in a large bowl. While whisking continuously, slowly add the oil. Whisk in the vinegar, followed by the salt, pepper, and poultry seasoning.

Place the chicken in an airtight container or zip-top bag and pour in the marinade. Cover the container or seal the bag and marinate in the refrigerator for 12 to 24 hours.

Preheat the oven to 450°F.

Combine the potatoes, zucchini, tomatoes, 2 tablespoons of the olive oil, the salt, and the pepper on a sheet pan and toss to coat. Remove the chicken from the marinade, shaking off any

excess, and nestle the chicken among the vegetables, skin-side up. Roast for 15 to 20 minutes. Reduce the heat to 400°F. Toss the vegetables, rotate the pan, and roast for another 20 minutes. Combine the corn and the remaining 1 tablespoon olive oil in a small bowl. Scatter the corn over the sheet pan and roast for another 5 to 10 minutes, until a kitchen thermometer inserted into the thickest part of a thigh registers 160°F. (If you're using a halved chicken, you may want to cook it for a bit longer; remove the vegetables from the sheet pan before doing so if they're already very well crisped and tender.)

Garnish with the basil (if using) and serve.

# muffuletta chicken rolls

Stuffed chicken breasts might sound a little dated, but who cares when they're stuffed with olive salad, provolone, and deli meats. Those are the components of a muffuletta, the famous Italian American sandwich of New Orleans, in which a stack of thinly sliced soppressata, mortadella, and capicola are also pressed inside a seeded roll. The Italian American grocery where it is said to have originated, Central Grocery, still commands long lines at the deli counter for that sandwich. My stance is that anything that unquestionably good is game for remaking, or at least affixing to something else. These boneless, skinless chicken breasts proudly wear a slice of salami like a dotted robe for a crispy surface, and it also helps to seal up the rolled chicken. It's okay if some of the rolls sputter and ooze a bit—the vegetables on the sheet pan won't mind marinating in the sweat of cheese and cured meats. So there's no actual muffuletta roll here, but the sandwich's signature olive salad is sprinkled about after roasting for a crisp, piquant topping. And, really, rolls are overrated anyway. **Serves 4**

4 pieces thin-sliced chicken breast, or 2 boneless, skinless whole breasts, butterflied and split

About 1 pound cauliflower florets, cut into pieces no thicker than 2 inches

1 pound carrots, halved lengthwise and cut into 2-inch sections

2 tablespoons extra-virgin olive oil

½ teaspoon salt

¼ teaspoon black pepper

**for the olive salad**

½ cup finely diced onion

½ cup roasted red peppers, chopped

1 cup green olives, pitted and coarsely chopped

1 teaspoon dried oregano

Handful of celery leaves, chopped (optional)

½ teaspoon red chile flakes (optional)

2 tablespoons extra-virgin olive oil

1 tablespoon red wine vinegar

4 slices Genoa salami

4 slices provolone cheese

Preheat the oven to 425°F.

Place one slice of chicken breast between two sheets of plastic wrap on a cutting board. Gently smack it all over with a meat tenderizer or the blunt end of a rolling pin, being careful not to tear it or break it up, until it has grown slightly larger in size. Repeat with the rest of the chicken slices.

Combine the cauliflower, carrots, olive oil, salt, and pepper on a sheet pan and toss to coat. Spread the vegetables into a single layer and roast for 10 minutes.

Meanwhile, make the olive salad: Combine the onion, peppers, olives, oregano, celery leaves (if using), chile flakes (if using), olive oil, and vinegar in a medium bowl.

Place one slice of the salami on a cutting board and lay a slice of the chicken on top, then a slice of the provolone, folding and tucking in the cheese so that it doesn't extend beyond the chicken. Scatter a tablespoon of the olive salad on top. Gently roll up the salami and the chicken breast to enclose the cheese and olive salad. Secure the roll with two toothpicks. Repeat to make three additional rolls; reserve the remaining olive salad for serving.

After roasting for 10 minutes, remove the sheet pan from the oven and toss the cauliflower and carrots. Add the chicken rolls to the sheet pan in a single layer. Roast for 15 to 20 minutes, until the salami has darkened and is becoming crispy and the vegetables are sufficiently crisp.

Scatter the remaining olive salad over the rolls and vegetables and serve.

# thai yellow curry chicken thighs
## with cucumber relish

Thai yellow curry, or kaeng kari, is one of the most popular types of Thai curries, along with green curry and red curry. It tends to be lower in heat, so it's great for the masses. I love Thai food, but I don't know my way around the Thai spice pantry too well—it feels like I'm always missing something I need in a recipe. Fortunately, Leela Punyaratabandhu set me straight on just what you need for an intensely flavorful, surprisingly simple, Thai yellow curry–seasoned sheet pan chicken. She should know—Leela's the author of three cookbooks: *Bangkok*, *Simple Thai Food*, and *Flavors of the Southeast Asian Grill*. I love how she marinates the chicken in fish sauce overnight, then utilizes an easy-to-find, premade (and legit delicious) curry paste and curry powder for a one-two punch of flavor. **Serves 6 to 8**

8 bone-in, skin-on chicken thighs

3 tablespoons fish sauce

2 teaspoons salt

3 tablespoons packed grated palm sugar, or 2 tablespoons packed light brown sugar

½ cup packed Thai yellow curry paste (Mae Ploy, Maesri, or any Thai brand)

½ cup unsweetened full-fat coconut milk

¾ pound waxy potatoes, such as new potatoes or Yukon Golds, cut into 2-inch cubes

¾ pound yellow or white onions, cut through the cores into 1-inch-wide (at the widest part) wedges

¼ cup coconut oil, melted, or vegetable oil

3 tablespoons Madras curry powder

**for the cucumber relish**

½ cup granulated sugar

½ cup distilled white vinegar

2 tablespoons water

¼ teaspoon salt

½ cup thinly sliced English or Persian cucumber

1 ounce shallot, thinly sliced lengthwise

1 red or green jalapeño or serrano pepper, thinly sliced crosswise

Cooked jasmine or sticky rice for serving

Put the chicken in a zip-top bag and add the fish sauce, 1 teaspoon of the salt, and the palm sugar. Seal the bag and massage the seasonings into the chicken. Marinate in the refrigerator for 24 hours.

Preheat the oven to 375°F. Whisk together the curry paste and coconut milk in a medium bowl until no lumps remain. Using a rubber spatula, scrape every bit of the mixture into the bag with the chicken. Seal the bag and knead until every chicken thigh is thoroughly coated with the curry paste mixture. Arrange the chicken thighs on a sheet pan, skin-side up. Drizzle any liquid left in the bag over them.

In a large bowl, toss the potatoes and onions with the remaining 1 teaspoon salt and the melted coconut oil. Arrange the vegetables in and around the chicken. Dust everything with curry powder. Roast for 30 minutes.

Make the cucumber relish: Combine the granulated sugar, vinegar, water, and salt in a small saucepan and bring to a boil over medium heat, stirring. Remove from the heat and let cool completely.

After roasting for 30 minutes, raise the oven temperature to 400°F, rotate the pan, and roast for another 20 to 25 minutes, until the chicken skin and vegetables are well browned and the potatoes are fork-tender.

Just before serving, combine the cucumber, shallot, and jalapeño in a medium bowl and pour the cooled syrup over them; mix well.

Serve the chicken, potatoes, and onions over warm jasmine or sticky rice, drizzled with the pan juices, with cucumber relish on the side.

# oaxacan chicken
## with oregano and garlic

My summers are so indebted to Pati Jinich, the award-winning cooking show host and cookbook author. I've got her simple, essential salsa recipes from *Pati's Mexican Table* pretty much memorized, which is immensely helpful when I have too many tomatoes. Pati, of course, has a lot more chops in the kitchen than salsa, and for this book, she kindly offered up this recipe for zesty, oregano-rubbed Oaxacan-style roasted chicken, which was featured on an episode of her PBS show. In this region of southern Mexico, the most culturally diverse in the country, you can find this type of roast chicken in homes and at fondas, or small restaurants. Pati says that her boys adore this chicken, and she loves it, too, not only for the flavors but also because it reminds her that an incredibly simple dish like this can come from such an incredibly complex cuisine. It sounds like a crazy amount of garlic—and it is!—but it doesn't taste too garlicky in the end. After marinating along with the oregano and lime juice, it all melds into one amazing roast chicken. **Serves 6 to 8**

40 garlic cloves, peeled

1½ cups fresh oregano leaves, plus a few more for garnish

¾ cup extra-virgin olive oil

⅓ cup fresh lime juice

2½ teaspoons salt, plus more as needed

¾ teaspoon black pepper, plus more as needed

3 pounds bone-in, skin-on chicken parts, or 1 (3½- to 4-pound) whole chicken, spatchcocked (see page 24)

2 pounds baby red potatoes, halved or quartered (no pieces thicker than 2 inches)

2 pounds carrots, cut into 1-inch sections

2 red onions, quartered

2½ cups chicken stock

**NOTE** You will need two half sheet pans to prepare this dish.

Preheat the oven to 450°F.

In a food processor or molcajete, combine the garlic, oregano, ½ cup of the olive oil, the lime juice, 1½ teaspoons of the salt, and ¼ teaspoon of the pepper and process or mash until coarse and well mixed but not completely pureed.

Place the chicken in a large bowl or casserole dish. Rub the garlic mixture all over the chicken, cover, and marinate in the refrigerator for at least 2 hours or up to 24 hours.

Combine the potatoes, carrots, onions, and the remaining ¼ cup olive oil, 1 teaspoon salt, and ½ teaspoon pepper on a sheet pan and toss to combine. Transfer half the vegetables to another sheet pan. If you're using chicken parts, divide

them evenly between the pans and arrange them skin-side up, nestled in the vegetables. If using a whole spatchcocked chicken, move most of the vegetables to the second sheet pan and place the chicken in the center, with the remaining vegetables surrounding it.

Roast for 15 minutes, then remove the sheet pans from the oven and reduce the oven temperature to 375°F. Pour half the stock onto each pan and roast for another 45 minutes, or until the chicken is cooked through and the juices run clear when it is pierced with a knife.

Scatter some additional oregano leaves over the top and serve.

# nashville-style hot chicken
## with bacon collard greens

Purists, beware: This rendition of Nashville hot chicken is not deep-fried, as the beloved dish is traditionally prepared. But it's still as spicy, tangy, and chicken-y as the original, and I've made you some bacon-flecked collard greens to serve on the side, so what's there to complain about? The legend behind Nashville hot chicken involves a failed revenge plot: An angry wife wanted to spike some fried chicken with enough cayenne pepper to make her cheating husband choke. Instead, he loved it. Nashville hot chicken is usually prepared with a fiery marinade enriched with buttermilk, which helps tenderize the chicken while it soaks overnight. Because I can never use up buttermilk when I buy it, I've substituted plain yogurt instead, which also has enzymes to help tenderize the meat. Please go get the biggest bottle of hot sauce you can find—Louisiana-style Crystal hot sauce and Frank's RedHot are good choices—not a wimpy dropper-size one of that other unnamed brand. This recipe uses a lot of it. **Serves 4 to 6**

### for the marinade

1 cup plain yogurt (not Greek-style)

1 cup vinegar-based red hot sauce, such as Crystal or Frank's RedHot

1 teaspoon cayenne pepper

1 tablespoon garlic powder, or 3 garlic cloves, smashed

1 teaspoon onion powder, or ¼ cup chopped onion

½ teaspoon paprika

1 teaspoon black pepper

1 tablespoon salt

2½ to 3 pounds bone-in, skin-on chicken pieces (thighs, legs, drumsticks, breasts, or whole wings)

1 pound sweet potatoes, ends trimmed, quartered lengthwise, and chopped into wedges no thicker than 1 inch

3 tablespoons extra-virgin olive oil

Salt and black pepper

4 to 6 large collard green leaves, thick ribs removed and shredded

1 small onion, sliced

2 slices bacon, cut crosswise into 1-inch-wide pieces

Make the marinade: Combine the yogurt, hot sauce, cayenne pepper, garlic powder, onion powder, paprika, black pepper, and salt in an airtight container or zip-top bag.

Add the chicken to the marinade, cover the container or seal the bag, and marinate in the refrigerator for 12 to 24 hours.

Preheat the oven to 425°F.

Remove the chicken pieces from the marinade, shaking off any excess, and arrange them on a sheet pan. Toss the sweet potatoes, 1 tablespoon of the olive oil, ¼ teaspoon salt, and a generous pinch of black pepper in a large bowl. Place the sweet potatoes cut-side down on the sheet pan in a single layer, around and between the chicken. Roast for 20 minutes.

Meanwhile, in the bowl you used for the sweet potatoes, combine the collard greens, onion, bacon, the remaining 2 tablespoons olive oil, ¼ teaspoon salt, and ¼ teaspoon black pepper and toss to combine.

After roasting for 15 to 20 minutes, flip the sweet potatoes and make room on the pan for the collard green mixture. Roast for another 20 minutes, or until a kitchen thermometer inserted into the thickest part of a thigh registers 160°F and the collard green mixture is crispy and lightly browned. Remove the pan from the oven and serve.

# jamaican ginger beer chicken
## with squash and brussels sprouts

The neighborhood of Brooklyn I've lived in for the past twelve years has a strong West Indies culture, and I'm blessed to walk by shops selling Caribbean produce like cassava roots and specialties like homemade beef patties (a turmeric-stained pastry with piping-hot spiced meat inside) and fresh fruit or aloe juices every day. In the summertime, people break out their oil drums to smoke jerk chicken on the street for friends and family—and the lucky neighbor. While that smoke from an outside grill is crucial to a proper jerk chicken, I love the varied ingredients typical of a jerk chicken marinade, like ginger, fresh thyme, Scotch bonnet chiles, soy sauce, brown sugar, and citrus juice. This is not typical of any jerk chicken preparations that I've seen, but I gave mine a sticky glaze by spilling some high-quality ginger beer on the bottom of the pan toward the end of cooking. The glaze gets all over the vegetables, too; feel free to change up the ones I've called for here for your favorites, like cauliflower or broccoli, instead. **Serves 4**

### for the marinade

2 garlic cloves, smashed

1 (2-inch) piece fresh ginger, peeled and sliced

2 scallions, chopped

½ cup soy sauce

2 tablespoons fresh lime juice

1 tablespoon fresh thyme leaves

1 Scotch bonnet pepper, seeded, or 2 or 3 fresh jalapeños, seeded

½ teaspoon allspice

1 tablespoon salt

½ cup packed brown sugar

2 pounds bone-in chicken thighs or drumsticks

1 pound winter squash, such as acorn or butternut, halved, seeded, and cut into 1- to 2-inch cubes or wedges, or 1 pound summer squash or zucchini, halved lengthwise and cut crosswise into 2-inch-wide pieces

½ pound brussels sprouts, halved (optional)

2 tablespoons neutral oil, such as grapeseed

½ teaspoon salt

¼ teaspoon black pepper

1½ cups ginger beer, such as Reed's

Crispy Kale Crown (page 29; optional)

2 scallions, chopped

Fresh thyme leaves, for garnish

Lime wedges, for serving

Make the marinade: Combine the garlic, ginger, scallions, soy sauce, lime juice, thyme, Scotch bonnet pepper, allspice, salt, and brown sugar in a blender and blend until smooth.

Place the chicken in an airtight container or zip-top bag and pour in the marinade. Cover the container or seal the bag and marinate in the refrigerator for at least 12 hours or up to 48 hours.

Preheat the oven to 450°F.

Combine the squash, brussels sprouts (if using), neutral oil, salt, and black pepper in a large bowl and toss to coat. Arrange the squash and brussels sprouts on a sheet pan in a single layer, cut-side down.

Remove the chicken from the marinade, shaking off any excess, and arrange them around and on top of the vegetables. Roast for 20 minutes. Flip and toss the vegetables around and rotate the pan. If adding the Crispy Kale Crown, add it now, according to the directions on page 29. Roast for another 10 to 15 minutes, until the squash pieces are tender throughout. Pour the ginger beer onto the sheet pan and roast for another 5 minutes, or until the ginger beer is bubbling.

Scatter the scallions and some fresh thyme leaves over the chicken and vegetables. Serve with lime wedges on the side.

# miso-marinated chicken
## with crispy brussels sprouts, baby turnips, and apples

Marinating a fatty fish like salmon or mackerel in miso paste for one or two days before broiling it is a plan-ahead flex in my kitchen. The formula works amazingly well for chicken thighs and legs, too, with the dark meat absorbing all the flavors of the simple marinade. As proof of the powers of an overnight marinade, you rinse off all the paste before cooking this chicken (it'll burn on the surface otherwise) but can still really taste the slightly sweet, generously salty, and deep umami flavor that has penetrated the meat throughout. I like surrounding this exceptionally delicious chicken with some bitter vegetables like brussels sprouts and turnips and crisp apples to bring out the sweetness for a finishing touch. Try it with another combo of vegetables, too. If you're looking for a bit more sauciness, I've included an optional bright sauce or dressing to serve with the dish. **Serves 4 to 6**

¼ cup white miso paste (shiro miso)

1 tablespoon rice vinegar

1 tablespoon mirin

1 tablespoon sugar

6 bone-in, skin-on chicken thighs, drumsticks, or boneless thighs

3 tablespoons neutral oil

10 to 12 brussels sprouts, halved

6 to 8 small Hakurei turnips or Sparkler radishes, halved

1 medium onion, halved and thinly sliced

¼ teaspoon salt

**for the miso-shallot dressing (optional)**

2 tablespoons white miso paste (shiro miso)

¼ cup rice vinegar

¼ cup finely chopped shallot

1 tablespoon honey, or more to taste

1 tablespoon water

2 teaspoons toasted sesame oil

1 large apple, peeled, cored, and cut into thin matchsticks

Combine the miso paste, vinegar, mirin, and sugar in a small bowl. Rub the miso mixture over the chicken to coat thoroughly. Transfer to an airtight container or zip-top bag and marinate in the refrigerator for at least 12 hours or up to 24 hours.

Preheat the oven to 450°F.

Rinse the chicken to remove all the miso mixture and pat it dry. Coat the chicken with 1 tablespoon of the neutral oil.

Combine the brussels sprouts, turnips, onion, the remaining 2 tablespoons neutral oil, and the salt on a large sheet pan and toss to coat. Arrange the turnip halves cut-side down in a single layer on one end of the pan. Place the brussels sprouts cut-side down in a single layer in the center of the pan. Place the chicken skin-side up on the other side of the pan. (This arrangement helps contain the juices from the chicken to one side, so that many of the vegetables stay relatively dry and get crisp.) Nestle the onion snugly between the chicken pieces. Roast for 20 minutes, then flip any vegetables that are well browned on the bottom and scatter them around on the pan. Rotate the pan and roast for another 5 to 10 minutes if using boneless thighs, or 20 to 25 minutes if using bone-in pieces, until a kitchen thermometer inserted into the thickest part of a thigh registers 160°F.

Meanwhile, make the miso-shallot dressing (if using): Combine the miso paste, rice vinegar, shallot, honey, water, and sesame oil in a small bowl.

Drizzle the dressing over the sheet pan, top with the apples, and serve.

# saffron-marinated chicken
## with cherry tomatoes and scallions

Louisa Shafia, author of *The New Persian Kitchen,* is my Persian-cooking Yoda. Over an unforgettable multicourse meal, she once taught me how to prepare saffron-infused rice with tahdig, a crispy crust on the bottom of the pan. Here that saffron gets absorbed into the chicken for Louisa's sheet pan take on jujeh kabab, a classic Persian chicken kabob that is marinated in saffron and turmeric and traditionally served with a grilled tomato. According to Louisa, that overnight-saffron step not only flavors and colors the chicken but helps to tenderize it as well. Serve this dish with a fluffy grain like rice or any whole grain or quinoa (such as the Quinoa Pilaf with Chickpeas and Preserved Lemon on page 110). **Serves 4**

½ teaspoon saffron threads, ground (see Note)

2 tablespoons hot (not boiling) water

6 garlic cloves, minced

½ cup fresh lemon juice

1 cup full-fat plain yogurt

1 teaspoon ground turmeric

Salt and black pepper

4 bone-in, skin-on chicken thighs

2 bunches scallions, white and green parts separated

2 quarts cherry tomatoes

4 tablespoons extra-virgin olive oil

**NOTE** Saffron yields more flavor and color when it's ground and steeped in warm liquid. To grind saffron strands, combine them with a dash of salt or sugar and pulverize them using a mortar and pestle or a spice grinder, or put them in a small glass jar and use the round end of a wooden spoon handle to crush the saffron against the sides of the jar.

Put the ground saffron in a small bowl, add the hot water, and let it steep for 15 minutes.

In a large bowl, whisk together the saffron-infused water, garlic, lemon juice, yogurt, and turmeric. Add 1 tablespoon salt and several grinds of black pepper. Taste the marinade and adjust the seasoning with more salt and pepper, if necessary. It should be very flavorful and tart.

Pat the chicken thighs dry and arrange them in a shallow dish in a single layer. Pour the marinade over the thighs and toss a few times until they're well coated. Cover and refrigerate overnight.

Preheat the oven to 450°F.

Thinly slice the scallion greens and set them aside in a small bowl. Coarsely chop the scallion whites and put them in a large bowl. Add the cherry tomatoes, 2 tablespoons of the olive oil, a dash

of salt, and several grinds of pepper. Toss well to coat, then scrape everything onto a sheet pan and shake to distribute the tomatoes evenly.

Toss the chicken thighs in the marinade to make sure they're coated, then place them skin-side up on top of the tomatoes, spacing them evenly apart. Drizzle with the remaining 2 tablespoons olive oil and season lightly with salt and pepper.

Roast the chicken for 25 minutes, then rotate the pan and roast for another 20 minutes, or until a thermometer inserted in the thickest part of the thigh registers 160°F and the cherry tomatoes have released a lot of liquid into the pan.

Gently tilt the pan, scoop up a few spoonfuls of the liquid, and add it to the bowl with the scallion greens to wilt them. Spoon the scallion mixture over the chicken and tomatoes and serve.

# mom's soy sauce chicken
## with pineapple and bok choy

A reddish-stained, soy sauce–marinated chicken is one that's infused with loads of salty, fermented umami—and when you roast it with the skin on, you get even more umami from the crispy skin. These flavor bombs were invented by my mom and eight zillion other people who also know that soy sauce and chicken just go together. It's not really fair to give her full credit, but I will anyway. Here, instead of grilling, we're throwing them on a sheet pan to crisp alongside some bok choy, which, in my mom's kitchen, is commonly braised. In Taiwan, where my mom is from, pineapples are plentiful, and they're used in everything from chicken soups to fermented sauces. One key ingredient here is dark soy sauce, a more intense, concentrated type of soy sauce that will stain chicken a deeper shade of maroon when marinated overnight. You can find it in Asian groceries—or heap on some more light soy sauce if you can't. Scoop this dish over a bowl of sticky rice (page 118), ham fried rice (page 112), or sesame noodles (page 113). **Serves 4**

**for the marinade**

½ cup soy sauce

1 tablespoon dark soy sauce (or an additional 2 tablespoons soy sauce)

½ teaspoon salt

½ teaspoon white pepper

2 tablespoons toasted sesame oil

4 scallions, chopped

1 (2-inch) piece fresh ginger, peeled and thinly sliced

2 pounds bone-in, skin-on chicken pieces

3 small heads baby bok choy, halved

2 tablespoons neutral oil, such as grapeseed

¼ teaspoon salt

2 cups fresh pineapple chunks

2 scallions, chopped

Crispy Chile Oil (page 128; optional)

Make the marinade: Combine the soy sauce, dark soy sauce, salt, white pepper, sesame oil, scallions, and ginger in an airtight container or zip-top bag.

Add the chicken to the marinade, cover the container or seal the bag, and marinate in the refrigerator for 12 to 24 hours.

Preheat the oven to 425°F.

Combine the baby bok choy, 1 tablespoon of the neutral oil, and the salt on a sheet pan and toss to coat. Arrange the bok choy cut-side down. Toss the pineapple chunks with the remaining 1 tablespoon neutral oil and scatter the pineapple around the pan.

Remove the chicken pieces from the marinade, shaking off any excess, and arrange them on the sheet pan nestled among the bok choy and pineapple. Roast for 25 to 30 minutes, then check on the bok choy; flip them or remove them from the sheet pan if they're sufficiently crisped. Rotate the pan and roast for another 10 minutes, until a kitchen thermometer inserted into the thickest part of a piece registers 160°F.

Sprinkle with the scallions and Crispy Chile Oil (if using) and serve.

# turmeric chicken
## with curry leaf masala roasted vegetables

I love tasting the evolution of immigrant cuisines in America, whether it's from home cooks like my mom or acclaimed restaurant chefs who are creatively tapping into the various influences in their lives. San Francisco chef Preeti Mistry is a champion of subverting tradition in favor of flavors that are authentic to her—as well as incredibly delicious. Her cookbook, *The Juhu Beach Club*, beautifully illustrates that journey and how her Indian American upbringing has manifested in an exciting cuisine. In Preeti's colorful, sheet-pan ready recipe (see photo on pages 96–97), the chicken is soaked overnight in a spiced yogurt marinade before roasting; the flavors of the spices infuse the chicken, and the yogurt helps to tenderize the meat. **Serves 6 to 8**

**for the marinade**

3 tablespoons coriander seeds, or 2 tablespoons ground coriander

1 tablespoon cumin seeds, or 1 teaspoon ground cumin

1 cup full-fat plain yogurt (not Greek-style)

2 tablespoons salt

2 tablespoons minced fresh ginger

2 tablespoons minced garlic

1 teaspoon ground turmeric

1 teaspoon Indian red chile powder or cayenne pepper

Juice of 2 lemons (about ½ cup)

2 tablespoons cold water

1 (3- to 4-pound) whole chicken, or 3 to 4 pounds bone-in, skin-on legs and/or breasts

1 pound baby potatoes, 1 to 2 inches in diameter, halved (or quartered if larger)

1 pound rainbow carrots, diced

1 medium red onion, diced large

1 pound brussels sprouts or baby turnips, halved or quartered if large

1 cup lightly packed fresh or dried curry leaves (these can be ordered online)

2 tablespoons minced fresh ginger

1 teaspoon brown mustard seeds

¼ cup neutral oil, such as grapeseed

1 teaspoon ground turmeric

1 teaspoon salt

4 tablespoons unsalted butter, melted

> **NOTE** You will need two half sheet pans to prepare this dish.

Make the marinade: If using whole coriander and cumin seeds, finely grind them in a spice grinder, then transfer to a medium bowl. Add the yogurt, salt, ginger, garlic, turmeric, chile powder, lemon juice, and water and whisk to combine.

If using a whole chicken, to spatchcock it, place it breast-side down on a cutting board. Using kitchen scissors (if you have a cleaver or sharp chef's knife, you can use that—carefully—instead), snip along each side of the spine to remove it. Flip the chicken breast-side up, place your palm on the center of the breast, and push down until you feel the breastbone crack. This should help the chicken lie flat.

Place the spatchcocked chicken or chicken pieces in a large airtight container or zip-top bag and pour in the marinade. Turn to coat it thoroughly in the marinade, then cover the container or seal the bag and marinate in the refrigerator for at least 4 hours or up to 12 hours.

Preheat the oven to 400°F.

Combine the potatoes, carrots, onion, brussels sprouts, curry leaves, ginger, mustard seeds, neutral oil, turmeric, and salt in a large bowl and toss to combine. Spread the veggies and seasonings over a sheet pan.

Remove the chicken from the marinade, shaking off any excess (or allow it to drip for a minute into the sink). If you're using a spatchcocked whole chicken, place it skin-side up in the center of a second sheet pan and transfer some of the vegetables to the pan with the chicken, arranging them around it; leave most of the vegetables on the other pan. If you're using chicken parts, transfer half the vegetables to a second sheet pan and nestle the chicken parts in the veggies, skin-side up, dividing the pieces evenly between the pans. Roast for 30 minutes, then toss or flip the vegetables and brush the melted butter all over the chicken. Roast for another 10 to 15 minutes, until the chicken skin is golden brown and a kitchen thermometer inserted into the thickest part of a thigh registers 160°F. Transfer to a serving dish and arrange the vegetables around the chicken to serve.

# puerto rican–vietnamese adobo chicken
## with roasted pineapple

It's worth seeking out lemongrass and yuzu juice (or sour orange juice) for the pungency they contribute to this sour, spicy, and slightly floral marinade for juicy chicken thighs. According to Von Diaz, author of the cookbook (and moving memoir) *Coconuts and Collards,* Puerto Rico shares a lot of favorite ingredients with Southeast Asia—including a love of chicken and rice; the use of fresh, pungent herbs like cilantro; and sour, tenderizing vinegar and citrus. With this in mind, Von created this sheet pan chicken recipe, which reflects both her Puerto Rican heritage and the fact that for the last decade, she's lived in US cities with large Southeast Asian communities. Her take on Puerto Rican chicken with adobo seasoning can be enjoyed as an entrée with rice (such as ham fried rice, page 112, or sticky rice, page 118) or on top of a green salad with lots of fresh cucumber. **Serves 4 to 6**

2 tablespoons chopped fresh lemongrass, or the zest of 2 lemons

1 tablespoon chopped fresh ginger

3 large garlic cloves

1½ teaspoons kosher salt

1 tablespoon rice vinegar

2 tablespoons bottled yuzu juice (can be in found Asian groceries) or sour orange juice (can be found in Latin groceries)

3 tablespoons chopped fresh cilantro, plus more for garnish

1 teaspoon mirin

6 boneless, skinless chicken thighs (about 1½ pounds)

6 to 8 orange, yellow, and/ or red baby bell peppers

1 tablespoon neutral oil, such as grapeseed

¼ teaspoon salt

2 cups fresh pineapple chunks

Lemon or lime wedges, for garnish

Combine the lemongrass, ginger, garlic, and kosher salt in a small food processor and pulse until well chopped, stopping to scrape down the sides with a spatula as needed. Add the vinegar, yuzu juice, cilantro, and mirin and process to incorporate fully, stopping to scrape the sides and lid. (Alternatively, mince the garlic, ginger, and lemongrass, then combine them in a medium bowl and whisk in the vinegar, yuzu juice, cilantro, and mirin until well combined.)

Dry the chicken thighs well with a paper towel, then place them in a large zip-top bag. Pour in the marinade and seal the bag, leaving a little air inside so the marinade can fully cover the chicken. Shake well and massage the marinade into the chicken, then marinate for at least 30 minutes or, preferably, in the refrigerator for 12 to 24 hours.

Preheat the broiler to low, with an oven rack positioned at least 7 inches below the heat source.

Combine the baby bell peppers, oil, and salt on a sheet pan and toss to coat. Remove the chicken thighs from the marinade, shaking off any excess, and place them flat on a sheet pan. Arrange the pineapple around and between the chicken. Broil for 8 minutes, then flip the chicken and peppers and raise the broiler heat to high. Broil for another 7 minutes, until the chicken thighs are deep brown with a bit of char around the edges, checking halfway through to ensure that the chicken isn't burning. If more char is desired, they can be left under the broiler for another 1 to 2 minutes.

Arrange the thighs on a serving dish with the peppers and pineapple. Garnish with fresh cilantro and serve with the lemon or lime wedges on the side.

# chicken saltimbocca, sheet pan–style

I've occasionally seen chicken or veal saltimbocca on Italian restaurant (or ristorante) menus, right up there with the Marsalas and Franceses, and assumed it was one of those American Italian classics with roots in southern Italy. Wrong. It's a Roman dish, which I learned about when reading *Olives & Oranges* by Sara Jenkins, the chef of the restaurants Porsena and Porchetta in New York City. The word *saltimbocca* means "leap in the mouth," and while the dish hasn't been leaping onto too many trendy restaurant menus in the last couple of decades, I love the prosciutto that coddles the boneless meat, crisping on the outside, and the white wine sauce made in the pan. I took my cues from Jenkins's recipe (hers made with veal instead of chicken) for this sheet pan version, which is a lot easier than flipping multiple batches of the meat bundles in a hot pan with oil splattering everywhere. Sara wrote that Romans will argue endlessly over whether the sage should be underneath the prosciutto or on the outside. Do whichever is easiest for you. Be sure to serve this with some crusty Italian bread to soak up the pan juices. **Serves 6 to 8**

1 pound very thinly sliced prosciutto (includes extra for cook's treats)

8 pieces thin-sliced chicken breasts, or 4 boneless, skinless whole breasts, butterflied and split

Salt and black pepper

16 whole fresh sage leaves, plus a few more, thinly sliced, for garnish

1 large zucchini, cut into 1-inch chunks, or 1½ to 2 cups of broccoli or cauliflower florets

2 cups halved or quartered cremini or button mushrooms

1 pint cherry or grape tomatoes, halved

4 to 5 tablespoons extra-virgin olive oil

½ cup dry white wine

2 tablespoons unsalted butter

Crusty Italian bread, for serving

Preheat the oven to 425°F.

Place 2 or 3 slices of prosciutto on a sheet pan and cover with one thin-sliced chicken breast. Sprinkle the top with a little salt and pepper. Roll up the breast so that the prosciutto is covering it completely (it's okay if you have some loose bits of prosciutto hanging off). Place 2 sage leaves on top of the roll and fasten them with a toothpick on the outside. (Alternatively, place the sage leaves on the prosciutto, then add the chicken and roll it up—see headnote.) Repeat to make 7 more rolls.

Toss the zucchini, mushrooms, and tomatoes on a sheet pan with 2 to 3 tablespoons of the oil, about ½ teaspoon salt, and ¼ teaspoon pepper. Arrange in a single layer and nestle the chicken rolls in between them on the sheet pan. Drizzle everything with another 1 to 2 tablespoons olive oil.

Roast for 20 to 30 minutes, until the prosciutto and vegetables are lightly browned. Pour the white wine over the sheet pan and return to the oven to cook another 10 minutes. Remove from the oven, add the butter evenly around on the sheet pan, and shake everything around. Garnish with extra sage leaves and serve with the crusty bread.

# sumac chicken
## with butternut squash, red onion, and tahini-yogurt sauce

If you've tried za'atar (like in Za'atar-Rubbed Chicken with Carrots, Beets, and Labne, page 69) and wanted more of that tart, lemony taste hiding underneath the dried herbs, sumac is what you're looking for. This burgundy powder from the fruit of the sumac plant is used liberally in kitchens throughout the Middle East, and like most spices, it doesn't get better with time, so use plenty of it while you've got it. It makes an exceptional seasoning for chicken, especially after allowing it to absorb rich olive oil overnight. Here I've also added Urfa biber (a dried Turkish chile) for a little heat and some tahini to finish. It's great with roasted butternut squash, but I found that the squash really wanted to be alone on a separate pan in order to brown, at least for the first half of cooking. Serve this dish with some couscous or another fluffy, quick-cooking grain (such as the Quinoa Pilaf with Chickpeas and Preserved Lemon on page 110) and some kind of light salad, like Garlicky Smashed Cucumbers (page 120). **Serves 4 to 6**

2 pounds bone-in, skin-on chicken parts (legs, thighs, drumsticks, breasts, or whole wings)

1 large red onion, halved and thinly sliced

2 garlic cloves, smashed

2 teaspoons ground sumac

½ teaspoon ground cumin

½ teaspoon Urfa biber (Turkish chile flakes) or red chile flakes (optional)

4 tablespoons extra-virgin olive oil

1½ teaspoons salt

½ teaspoon black pepper

1 lemon

2 pounds butternut squash (about 1 medium-small squash), peeled, seeded, and cut into chunks or wedges no thicker than 1 inch and no longer than around 2 inches

½ cup Good on Everything Tahini-Yogurt Sauce (page 124)

½ cup packed fresh cilantro, parsley, or mint leaves, chopped

**NOTE** You will need two half sheet pans to prepare this dish.

In a large bowl, combine the chicken, sliced onion, smashed garlic, 1 teaspoon of the sumac, the cumin, urfa biber, 2 tablespoons of the oil, 1 teaspoon of the salt, ¼ teaspoon of the black pepper, 1 teaspoon lemon zest, and 1 tablespoon fresh lemon juice (using half the lemon) and toss. Cover with plastic (or transfer to an airtight plastic bag) and chill 12 hours.

Preheat the oven to 450°F.

Toss the butternut squash chunks with the remaining 2 tablespoons olive oil, ½ teaspoon salt, and ¼ teaspoon black pepper and spread onto a sheet pan in a single layer. Make sure that each squash piece gets full contact with the pan and has enough space, preferably at least ½ inch

in between, so that they can brown. Arrange the chicken, skin-side up, on another sheet pan and scatter the onions around and in between.

Roast for 20 minutes. Give the onions a toss and transfer the butternut squash to the sheet pan around the chicken and onions (they should be nicely browned). Roast for another 10 to 15 minutes, or until the chicken skin is golden brown and a kitchen thermometer registers 160°F when inserted into the thigh.

Drizzle the tahini-yogurt sauce over everything and sprinkle with the remaining 1 teaspoon sumac. Scatter the fresh herbs over the top and serve with the remaining lemon half on the side, for spritzing over the chicken as desired.

# deconstructed chicken-eggplant parm
with garlic toasts

Next to lasagna, chicken Parm and eggplant Parm belong on Italian American cooking's greatest hits playlist (and that's "Parm" short for Parmesan, not Parmigiano Reggiano, as this isn't sophisticated, continental Italian cooking but down-home Italian American). But unlike lasagna (the topic of *TASTE*'s first cookbook, released in 2019), Parm has stagnated, its formula rarely futzed with or elaborated upon in different ways. So here was the perfect challenge: find a way to, if not faithfully re-create, then make something that was reminiscent of the cheesy, bready, red-sauce-y classics on a sheet pan—with an eye on being efficient. Because deep-frying or pan-frying breaded chicken and eggplant slabs in batches is pretty taxing, I skipped the breading altogether in favor of using slabs of bread as the base for a stack of roasted eggplant and boneless chicken, which crisp on the bottom. To be clear, this is not your Nonna's classic chicken or eggplant Parm, but it's a great stand-in if you can't get to her house as often as you'd like. **Serves 4 to 6**

**for the tomato sauce (see notes)**

1 (28-ounce) can whole peeled plum tomatoes, with their juices

2 tablespoons extra-virgin olive oil

4 garlic cloves, minced

Pinch of red chile flakes (optional)

¼ teaspoon salt

¼ teaspoon black pepper

1 medium-large Italian eggplant, sliced lengthwise 1 inch thick

2 teaspoons salt

About 8 tablespoons extra-virgin olive oil

2 tablespoons salted butter, at room temperature

2 garlic cloves, minced

1 teaspoon dried oregano

8 (½- to 1-inch-thick) slices ciabatta or peasant bread, roughly the size of your chicken cutlets

½ teaspoon black pepper

4 pieces thinly sliced boneless chicken cutlets (about 1½ pounds total)

8 ounces fresh mozzarella cheese, sliced into ½-inch-thick rounds

¼ cup grated Parmesan cheese

½ cup fresh parsley leaves, chopped

**NOTES** You will need two half sheet pans to prepare this dish.

You can skip the tomato sauce, if you like, and substitute 4 cups store-bought marinara sauce.

Make the sauce: Pour the canned tomatoes and their juices into a large bowl and crush them well by hand.

Heat the olive oil in a small saucepan over medium-high heat. Add the garlic and chile flakes (if using) and cook until very fragrant, 10 to 20 seconds. Add the crushed tomatoes and their juices. Stir in the salt and black pepper and bring to a boil. Reduce the heat to low or medium-low so the sauce is bubbling consistently and cover. Check on the sauce every 10 minutes or so and give it a stir.

Lay the eggplant slices flat on a cutting board and sprinkle the surface of each with a generous pinch of salt, using up about 1 teaspoon of the salt. Let sit for 15 minutes.

Preheat the oven to 425°F. Grease two sheet pans well with olive oil, using 2 to 3 tablespoons of the oil on each.

Combine the butter, garlic, and ½ teaspoon of the oregano in a small bowl. Spread the butter mixture on the top of the bread slices and place the slices buttered-side up in a single layer on one of the prepared sheet pans.

Pat dry any droplets of moisture that have risen to the surface of the eggplant slices and arrange the eggplant in a single layer on the second prepared sheet pan. Drizzle the tops of the eggplant with a couple tablespoons of the olive oil and season with ¼ teaspoon of the black pepper. Transfer both sheet pans to the oven and roast for 5 minutes. Remove the pan with the bread from the oven and set aside. Flip the eggplant slices and roast for another 15 minutes.

Meanwhile, rub the chicken cutlets with 1 to 2 tablespoons olive oil and the remaining 1 teaspoon salt, ½ teaspoon oregano, and ¼ teaspoon black pepper.

After roasting for 20 minutes, remove the eggplant from the oven. Place a slice of eggplant on each slice of bread. Place a seasoned chicken cutlet on top of four of them. Top all the stacks with a slice of mozzarella and a ladleful (about ½ cup) of the tomato sauce. Roast for 20 to 30 minutes, until the cheese is totally melted and oozing. To check the doneness of the chicken, cut the thickest chicken Parm in half; if the meat is completely white throughout, it's ready to serve.

Sprinkle all over with the grated Parmesan and fresh parsley. Serve with any extra sauce alongside.

# three-cup chicken wings
## with eggplant and basil

This chicken marinade is based on the flavors of Three-Cup Chicken, a signature Taiwanese dish of bone-in chunks of dark meat chicken braised with soy sauce, rice wine, and sesame oil (the "three cups" in question), with copious ginger, garlic, and fresh basil to finish. It's the dish that most badgered me into embarking on a years-long mission to write a cookbook about Taiwanese food. And when that book, *The Food of Taiwan*, finally came out in 2015, it was one of the first dishes I wanted to re-create for pop-up book events. Going for snackable bites, I coated marinated party wings (which approximate the size of the bone-in chicken chunks that are traditionally braised in the dish) in a sweet-savory glaze made with the leftover marinade. In Taiwan's night markets and casual restaurants, you can find a lot of braised eggplant dishes, too, so I added some Asian eggplant to the pan. Showered with fresh herbs and crispy fried shallots, these commonly braised dishes travel well to the sheet pan. **Serves 4**

### for the marinade

¾ cup soy sauce

½ cup rice wine or sake

¼ cup toasted sesame oil

½ cup packed brown sugar

1 teaspoon red chile flakes (optional)

2 scallions, cut into 1- to 2-inch-long segments

1 (4-inch) piece fresh ginger, peeled and cut into 12 slices

About 12 garlic cloves, smashed

2 pounds party wings

2 large or 3 medium Asian eggplants, halved lengthwise

2 tablespoons neutral oil, such as grapeseed

Salt

1 tablespoon cornstarch

½ cup cold water

½ cup packed fresh Thai basil leaves

2 scallions, sliced

¼ cup store-bought fried shallots

Crispy Chile Oil (page 128; optional)

Steamed rice, for serving

Make the marinade: Combine the soy sauce, rice wine, sesame oil, brown sugar, and chile flakes (if using) in a medium bowl and stir to dissolve the sugar. Add the scallions, ginger, and garlic.

Place the chicken in an airtight container and pour in the marinade. Cover the container and marinate in the refrigerator for at least 12 hours or up to 48 hours, turning the chicken once or twice to ensure that the marinade is evenly distributed.

Preheat the oven to 450° F. Combine the eggplant halves, neutral oil, and a couple pinches of salt and arrange cut-side down on a sheet pan. Remove the chicken wings from the marinade, shaking off any excess, and arrange them between and around the eggplant halves. Transfer the marinade to a small saucepan.

Roast for 20 minutes, then carefully flip the eggplant over and rotate the pan. Roast for another 10 minutes, or until the wings are crisp and the eggplant is well softened.

Meanwhile, in a small bowl, whisk together the cornstarch with the cold water. Bring the marinade to a boil, then stir in the cornstarch mixture and return the marinade to a boil, stirring frequently as it thickens. Remove from the heat. Taste the sauce for seasoning; you may want to add a touch of water if it's too salty. Add half the basil to the sauce, stir, and let it wilt.

Drizzle the sauce over the sheet pan, sprinkle with the remaining basil, the scallions, the fried shallots, and Crispy Chile Oil (if using) and serve with the steamed rice.

# roasted dry-brined whole chicken
## with cherry-walnut stuffing

While a whole chicken with its backbone in place isn't as quick to cook as a spatchcocked bird, leaving it whole gives you the benefit of its cavity—a convenient place to park a halved head of garlic, a lemon, a bouquet of aromatic herbs, or some seasoned cubes of days-old bread. This chicken cave becomes a castle of dripping schmaltz for bread to soak up, so if you have the time to stuff and roast the whole bird, it makes a lot of sense to do so. An overnight dry brine is one way to future-proof crispy skin. This stuffing mixture is loosely based on the recipe that my father's family always used for their Thanksgiving turkey, which looks to be loosely based on the recipe that's found on the side of the colorful cardboard package for Bell's Seasoning brand poultry seasoning. So it's pretty old school, WASP-y American cooking, served with a salad incorporating some of the brighter elements of that stuffing, like apple and orange. Make this dish instead of turkey for Thanksgiving, if you're serving a small crowd. Or serve it in May for any (lucky) crowd. **Serves 6 to 8**

1 (3½- to 4-pound) whole chicken

2½ teaspoons salt

1 teaspoon black pepper

1½ to 2 pounds small red or Yukon Gold potatoes, halved

2 tablespoons extra-virgin olive oil

### for the stuffing

8 tablespoons (1 stick) unsalted butter

1 large onion, chopped

2 celery stalks, chopped

8 to 10 fresh sage leaves, thinly sliced

1 tablespoon fresh thyme leaves

2 to 3 rosemary sprigs (optional)

1 teaspoon orange zest

¼ teaspoon ground or freshly grated nutmeg

3 cups cubed stale bread, preferably French bread or another crusty, artisanal bread (it's perfectly fine to use rye, sourdough, or another flavorful bread, as long as you like the flavor)

1 teaspoon salt

½ teaspoon black pepper

¾ cup coarsely chopped walnuts

⅓ cup chopped dried cherries or another dried fruit, such as cranberries

½ large tart apple, such as Granny Smith, peeled, cored, and cubed

2 sliced orange rounds

### for the salad

4 cups mixed baby greens, such as arugula

¼ cup walnuts, toasted

½ an apple, cored and thinly sliced or cut into thin matchsticks (optional)

¼ cup dried cherries or another dried fruit

1 tablespoon extra-virgin olive oil

½ teaspoon Dijon mustard

1 teaspoon red wine vinegar

Salt and black pepper

Thinly sliced orange rounds for serving

### for the pan sauce

¼ cup dry white wine

1 cup hot water

Salt and black pepper

1 tablespoon butter

Rub the chicken all over with 2 teaspoons of the salt and 1 teaspoon of the pepper. Refrigerate, uncovered, overnight to help dry out the bird and promote crisp skin.

Make the stuffing: Melt 4 tablespoons of the butter in a large saucepan over medium-high heat. Add the onion and celery and cook, stirring, for 5 minutes. Add the sage, thyme, rosemary (if using), orange zest, and nutmeg. Add the remaining 4 tablespoons butter and let it sizzle with the herbs for 2 minutes. Remove from the heat. Fold in the cubed bread (you may want to transfer the mixture to a large bowl). Stir in the salt and pepper, the walnuts, the dried cherries, and the apple cubes.

Preheat the oven to 450°F.

Toss the potatoes with olive oil and the remaining ½ teaspoon salt on a sheet pan. Arrange in a single layer around the edges of the pan.

Carefully fill the cavity of the chicken with the stuffing, pressing down to pack as much as you can inside. Run your fingers inside the chicken's skin at its neck opening to release the skin from the top portion of the breast, being careful not to break the skin. If you have leftover stuffing, carefully pack it under the skin. Place an orange slice over each opening to the cavity. Truss the bird by tying its legs together with kitchen twine.

Place the chicken breast-side up in the center of the sheet pan and roast for 45 minutes, stopping to flip the potatoes and baste the chicken a couple of times with the pan juices. Reduce the oven temperature to 350°F and roast for 10 to 15 minutes more, until a kitchen thermometer inserted into the thickest part of a thigh registers 160°F and the juices from a pierced thigh run clear.

Make the salad: Combine the greens, walnuts, apple (if using), dried cherries, olive oil, mustard, vinegar, and a pinch of salt in a large bowl and toss to combine. Scatter the salad around the edges of a large serving platter and arrange the orange rounds around the sides. Arrange the roasted potatoes in the center of the platter.

Let the chicken cool at least 10 to 15 minutes before scooping out the stuffing into a serving bowl. Transfer the chicken to a cutting board and carve. Place the chicken pieces on the potatoes in the serving platter.

Meanwhile, make the pan sauce: Pour the wine over the sheet pan and scrape well to incorporate any flavorful clumps of browned crust into the liquid. Pour the hot water over the pan and transfer the mixture to a small saucepan. Bring to a boil for 5 to 6 minutes to cook off the alcohol and reduce to about ½ cup. If desired, pour the mixture through a strainer into a serving bowl to remove any lumps. Taste for seasoning and add salt and pepper as needed. Add the butter and stir to melt.

Serve the chicken and salad with the pan sauce on the side.

# 3

# chicken sidekicks

All right, here's the confession: not everything turns out awesome when roasted on a sheet pan. Green beans come out looking like elongated raisins. Cucumbers are best kept far from the oven. And sometimes you just want a grain-based side that can be quickly made on the stovetop while everything else is roasting. A crisp salad that wants nothing to do with roasting and flavor-packed starches that have no business in the oven are sometimes a chicken's best sidekicks. This section also includes a handful of sauces, some that were called out in recipes and others that *could* be drizzled on just about any of them, depending on your mood.

# quinoa pilaf
## with chickpeas and preserved lemon

The easiest pot of whole grains in my kitchen is actually not a grain at all, but a seed. I love how quickly you can make a fluffy pile of quinoa as a base for anything, and how you can extend it into a grain-salad-like meal. Here I've added some preserved lemon rind for a bit more piquancy than you can get from just straight-up fresh lemon juice, and bobs of chickpeas for more quick-and-easy protein. (You can buy preserved lemons in large supermarkets or online in jars. Or, if you have the time, it's easy to pack lemons with salt into a jar to preserve yourself.) To make this pilaf more of a whole meal, throw in some roasted squash, broccoli, cauliflower, or sweet potatoes and perhaps some fresh grape tomatoes and crumbled feta. **Serves 4**

4 cups cooked quinoa

⅓ cup finely chopped red onion

1 tablespoon capers (optional)

1 cup cooked or canned chickpeas, drained and rinsed well

½ cup fresh flat-leaf parsley leaves, chopped

3 to 4 tablespoons extra-virgin olive oil

1 tablespoon fresh lemon juice, plus more if needed

½ teaspoon salt, plus more if needed

¼ teaspoon black pepper, plus more if needed

1 tablespoon thinly sliced preserved lemon peel

In a large bowl, combine the quinoa, onion, capers (if using), chickpeas, parsley, olive oil, lemon juice, salt, pepper, and half of the preserved lemon peel. Mix well to combine thoroughly. Taste for seasoning and add extra salt, pepper, or lemon juice as desired. Sprinkle the remaining preserved lemon peel on top for garnish.

# anything goes fried rice
## with ham and peas

Fried rice and sticky rice dishes often follow the same principles: you toss in a little bit of animal fat, seasonings, and whatever odds and ends you may have left over or lying around to flavor a much greater mass of rice. But fried rice actually starts with a leftover: the rice itself. It's best to use day-old steamed rice for frying, since it will be drier and won't stick as easily (sorry, this doesn't work well with leftover sticky rice or glutinous rice). My mom used to add cubes of ham to her fried rice; I would not look down on you for adding Spam. I consider these proteins to be interchangeable extras, while scrambled eggs, green peas straight from the freezer, and chopped scallions are compulsory in fried rice for me. **Serves 4**

4 tablespoons neutral oil, such as grapeseed

About 4 ounces ham steak or Spam, diced

½ cup frozen peas

2 eggs, beaten

4 cups cooked rice, preferably dry, cold, and at least 1 day old or up to 5 days old

½ teaspoon white pepper, plus more if needed

½ teaspoon salt, plus more if needed

1 teaspoon soy sauce, or to taste

Dab of chile sauce or chile oil (such as Crispy Chile Oil, page 128; optional)

2 or 3 scallions, chopped

Heat 2 tablespoons of the neutral oil in a large, wide skillet, chef's pan, or wok over high heat. Once the oil is fairly hot, add the ham and stir to spread it over the pan, then sear, undisturbed, for about 30 seconds to lightly brown the bottom. Cook, stirring occasionally, for another 30 seconds, or until the ham is lightly browned all over. Add the peas to the pan and cook, stirring, for a minute to warm them through. Transfer the ham and peas to a bowl and set aside.

Heat the remaining 2 tablespoons neutral oil in the same pan over high heat. Beat the eggs again and pour them into the pan, stirring immediately to scramble them. Once the eggs are pretty much all scrambled, about 1 minute, transfer them to the bowl with the ham and peas. Turn off the heat.

Add the rice to the same pan and break apart any clumps. Season with the white pepper, salt, and soy sauce, adding it a few splashes at a time. Turn the heat back on to medium-high and stir to incorporate all the seasonings. Return the eggs, ham, and peas to the pan and stir to incorporate all the ingredients thoroughly. Taste for seasoning and add more salt, white pepper, or soy sauce as needed, as well as some chile sauce, if you like. Remove from the heat, stir in the scallions, and serve.

# simple sesame noodles
## with shredded vegetables

Before you think you need to go out to the Asian supermarket in order to make sesame noodles, check your pantry. There is no shame in using spaghetti or linguine instead of Chinese dried wheat noodles or peanut butter instead of Chinese toasted sesame paste to make this dish. That's the way my mom often made cold sesame noodles for barbecues and summer dinners. I find peanut butter is a much better substitute for Chinese sesame paste than tahini, because the peanuts are roasted first. This creates a much more robust flavor and darker color that's more similar to Chinese sesame paste than tahini, which is made with raw sesame seeds and is therefore paler. In Taiwan, packaged cold noodle meals like this one are sold at convenience stores, with the sauce and shredded vegetables in little compartments separate from the noodles, ready to toss together. Make it fresh, and use whatever variety of vegetables comes your way. **Serves 4 to 6**

**for the sauce**

¼ cup Chinese toasted sesame paste (can be found in Asian groceries) or creamy peanut butter

2 tablespoons soy sauce

2 tablespoons rice vinegar

2 tablespoons toasted sesame oil

2 tablespoons packed brown sugar

1 garlic clove, grated

1 to 2 teaspoons chile sauce or chile oil (such as Crispy Chile Oil, page 128; optional)

¼ cup water

Salt and white pepper (optional)

1 pound flat Chinese wheat noodles or linguine, cooked according to the package directions and drained

1 medium cucumber, julienned

1 medium carrot, julienned

4 radishes, julienned (optional)

1 cup snow peas, thinly sliced on a bias (optional)

4 scallions, chopped

1 tablespoon toasted sesame seeds (optional)

Make the sauce: In a large bowl, combine the sesame paste, soy sauce, vinegar, sesame oil, brown sugar, garlic, chile sauce (if using), and water and mix well to combine. Taste for seasoning and add salt and pepper or any more of the sauce ingredients, if desired.

Rinse the cooked noodles to remove excess starch or to cool them down if they've just been cooked. Place the noodles in a large bowl and toss with your hands to separate them.

You'll want to serve the noodles right after tossing them with the sauce, so wait until the last minute to combine them (otherwise, the noodles will absorb the sauce instead of being wet and saucy). Just before serving, pour the sauce over the noodles and toss with tongs to incorporate fully. Add the cucumber, carrot, radishes (if using), and snow peas (if using) and toss to combine.

Garnish with the scallions and sesame seeds, if desired, and serve.

# fresh tomato salad
## with sherry vinegar

This is the kind of salad that's just a showcase for the very best tomatoes you can find in late summer. While many cultures share a love of the simple summer tomato salad, the minimal seasonings of sherry vinegar and olive oil, along with thinly sliced onions, are a typical preparation for fresh tomatoes in Spanish and Basque cuisines. With its cheerful acidity and fruitiness, it brightens up any roast meat—like chicken. Step aside, balsamic vinegar. **Serves 4**

2 pounds beefsteak or heirloom tomatoes, thickly sliced

2 tablespoons Spanish sherry vinegar or red wine vinegar

2 to 3 tablespoons extra-virgin olive oil

Pinch of salt

Pinch of black pepper

1 small red onion, very thinly sliced

Arrange the tomato slices on a serving platter and drizzle with half of the vinegar and olive oil. Season with the salt and pepper. Scatter the onion slices all over and drizzle with the remaining vinegar and olive oil. Serve immediately.

# celery and watermelon radish salad
## with nuts and dried cherries

When you're facing a dearth of leafy greens that look fresh and bouncy, such as in the dead of winter, crisp celery stalks can be counted on for a great salad instead. Refreshing and flavorful, the stalks are sliced thinly on a bias and tossed with other firm veggies like radishes (or you can sub in carrots) for contrasting flavor and texture. If you like cooking chicken, chances are you'll have many of these types of vegetables lurking in your crisper, so wake them up in this vibrant salad with dried fruit, crunchy nuts, and a simple vinaigrette. **Serves 4 to 6**

**for the dressing**

1 tablespoon Dijon mustard

2 tablespoons apple cider vinegar

1 to 2 teaspoons pure maple syrup

¼ cup extra-virgin olive oil

Salt and black pepper

4 large celery stalks, and any fresh-looking leaves from the bunch

2 watermelon radishes, or 4 to 6 red Sparkler radishes

½ cup sweetened dried cherries or cranberries

½ cup of your favorite type of unsalted roasted nuts, coarsely chopped

Make the dressing: Whisk together the mustard, vinegar, and maple syrup in a small bowl. While whisking continuously, slowly drizzle in the olive oil and whisk until the mixture is thoroughly emulsified. Taste and season with salt and pepper.

Slice the celery stalks on a bias as thinly as you can into long blades. Slice the radishes crosswise as thinly as you can, or use a mandoline. Optionally, stack up the radish slices and sliver them into matchsticks.

Right before serving, combine the celery, radishes, and celery leaves in a serving bowl and toss with the dressing. Top with the dried cherries and the nuts and serve.

# sticky rice
## with leeks and shiitake mushrooms

Even though sticky rice is just a grain side dish, I find myself stuffing my face with it whenever I come across it. And when freshly made and spooned out piping hot, it's even more tempting. Leeks and shiitake mushrooms perfume the oil and the rice that's cooked in the same pot, and plenty of white pepper is infused throughout. Often in Chinese and Taiwanese sticky rice preparations, dried baby shrimp and sliced dry-cured sausage such as lap cheong are added. You can find both of these in Asian groceries; they're not essential, however, and leaving them out means this is a vegetarian-friendly side. **Serves 4 to 6**

¼ cup neutral oil, such as grapeseed

1 large leek, rinsed well and chopped

8 to 10 fresh shiitake mushrooms, thinly sliced, or dried shiitakes, fully reconstituted in water for 20 minutes and squeezed out (retain the soaking water if using dried shiitakes, and use this as part of the 3 cups of cooking water for the rice)

2 tablespoons dried baby shrimp, soaked in cold water for 10 minutes, drained, and chopped (optional)

½ teaspoon salt

½ teaspoon white pepper

2 cups short-grain glutinous rice (sometimes labeled "sweet rice" or "sushi rice")

3 cups water (or the amount of water called for on the package of rice)

2 tablespoons soy sauce

Heat the neutral oil in a medium-large pot with a lid over medium-high heat. Add the leek, shiitakes, and dried shrimp (if using) and cook for 2 minutes, then reduce the heat to low and cook, stirring occasionally, until the leeks are softened and translucent, about 5 minutes more.

Add the salt, white pepper, rice, water, and soy sauce and raise the heat to high to bring the water to a boil. Reduce the heat to maintain a gentle simmer and cover. Cook for 20 to 25 minutes, or following the instructions on the package of rice, until the rice is tender and the liquid has been fully absorbed. Check once or twice to ensure there is sufficient water and the bottom of the pot isn't scorching, and add more water if necessary.

Spoon the rice into a serving bowl. Alternatively, scoop the rice into a mixing bowl and pack it in. To serve, invert the bowl onto a plate so you have a mound of molded sticky rice.

# garlicky smashed cucumbers

Smacking logs of cucumbers with the side of a chef's knife is not just some kind of de-stressing hack. It's the best way to quickly break off the seed pockets—or at least most of them—and render the crisp flesh into irregular chunks to marinate. (See also Bang Bang Crispy Chicken, page 27, which follows a similar philosophy to attain just the right kind of brokenness in cooked chicken breasts.) This is a very simple recipe that you can expand on with further seasonings. If you like, try adding a bit of Crispy Chile Oil (page 128), or hold the sesame oil and make a panzanella when you have some leftover stale bread and tomatoes. **Makes 4 appetizer-size servings**

3 large cucumbers, peeled

1 teaspoon salt

2 garlic cloves, smashed and coarsely chopped

¼ teaspoon white pepper

¼ cup rice wine vinegar

1 tablespoon toasted sesame oil or olive oil, depending on what you're serving it with

**NOTE** Since you're removing the seeds anyway, it's perfectly fine to get regular cucumbers instead of fancier "seedless" types like English or Persian.

Cut the cucumber into thirds crosswise to create 2- to 3-inch-long cylindrical pieces. Place one piece of cucumber in the center of your cutting board and move the rest to the side. Smack the side of a wide chef's knife flat on the top of the cucumber, so that it breaks off into irregular chunks. Much of the seed pocket should have broken away from the flesh in the smash; discard this. Pick up the pieces of smashed cucumber and transfer them to a colander. Repeat with the rest of the cucumber. Break up any very large pieces of the smashed cucumber flesh so the pieces are all fairly uniform in size—it's fine if they're still irregular in shape. Set the colander in the sink. Season the cucumber all over with the salt and garlic, toss, and let stand for 30 minutes.

Toss the cucumbers and pat dry with paper towels. Transfer to a large bowl. Stir in the white pepper, vinegar, and sesame oil and serve.

# green bean "elotes"
## with cotija and lime

I really don't enjoy green beans after they've been baked or roasted—and you may have noticed that I didn't include them anywhere else in this book. Instead of coming out of the oven plump and crisp, they emerge wrinkled and deflated-looking, like a helium balloon that someone sucked too much out of to sound silly at a birthday party. Green beans are much better quickly sautéed. To beef them up a bit, I stole the concept for elotes, the Mexican street corn slathered with mayonnaise and liberally sprinkled with chile powder, lime juice, and crumbled cotija cheese. **Serves 4**

2 tablespoons extra-virgin olive oil

1 pound green beans, sliced into 1- to 2-inch-long pieces on a bias

Pinch of salt

Pinch of black pepper

1 lime, halved

¼ cup mayonnaise, sour cream, or crema (optional)

1 teaspoon chili powder

½ cup crumbled cotija cheese

Heat the olive oil over high heat in a cast-iron or other heavy-bottomed skillet. Once the oil begins to pop and sputter, add the green beans. Season with the salt and pepper and cook, stirring occasionally, for 2 minutes. Transfer to a serving plate.

Squeeze lime juice all over the green beans. Drizzle with the mayonnaise, if desired. Dust with the chili powder, top with the crumbled cotija, and serve.

# a very good citrus salad
## with olives, chiles, and mint

In the dead of winter, it can be hard to find a bright, refreshing salad to complement a meal. I have a solution: Grab a few winter citrus—blood orange, navel orange, pink or white grapefruit—and call it a day. And don't be shy with the fresh herbs like mint, parsley, cilantro, or dill. This mixture could also be tossed with some baby greens as part of a bigger salad, sparing you the need to use much dressing. **Serves 4**

1 large pink grapefruit

3 large navel oranges

2 blood oranges

2 tangerines or clementines

1 teaspoon red chile flakes

½ cup large green olives, pitted (see page 48)

2 tablespoons extra-virgin olive oil

¼ cup fresh mint, parsley, dill, cilantro, or basil leaves

**NOTE** You will need a very sharp knife to slice the citrus into rounds without squishing the fruit and releasing all their juice on your cutting board.

Trim the stem and blossom ends of the grapefruit to create two flat surfaces. Stand the fruit flat on a cutting board. Following the curve of the fruit, cut downward to remove the skin and white pith, removing as little of the flesh as possible. Turn the grapefruit on its side and slice it into thin rounds. Repeat with the navel oranges, blood oranges, and tangerines.

Arrange the grapefruit, orange, and tangerine rounds on a serving platter, laying them flat with some overlap. Scatter the chile flakes and olives over the top and drizzle with the olive oil. Garnish with the fresh mint and serve.

# good on everything
# tahini-yogurt sauce

I love making a simple tahini-lemon sauce without yogurt, and yogurt-lemon sauce without tahini, so consider this recipe a flexible suggestion, marrying the best of both worlds: nutty ground sesame paste and cooling yogurt. And it can be thinned to your preferred consistency with a splash of water, especially if you only have really thick Greek yogurt and it's just not happening when it comes to drizzling. This sauce works wonders on roasted vegetables, so it's used in a couple of recipes in this book—and it can go with many more. **Makes about ¾ cup**

¼ cup tahini

1 teaspoon lemon zest

1 tablespoon fresh
lemon juice

¼ cup yogurt

1 small garlic clove (or half
of one), finely grated

¼ teaspoon salt, plus more
if needed

Pinch of black pepper,
or to taste

1 tablespoon extra-virgin
olive oil, or more to taste

In a small bowl, combine the tahini, lemon zest, lemon juice, yogurt, garlic, salt, and pepper. Taste for seasoning and add more salt or pepper. Whisk in a tablespoon of olive oil. If desired, thin it out with a little water or just more olive oil. The sauce can be kept, refrigerated, for up to one week.

# creamy georgian walnut sauce

If you haven't made a walnut-based sauce before, you will be shocked (shocked!) at how easy it is to create a rich, nutty, and tangy sauce from little more than walnuts, garlic, water, and vinegar. Walnut-based sauces, and walnuts in general, play a big role in Georgian cuisine. They can also be found in other Eastern European and Middle Eastern dishes, like the Turkish sauce tarator, which usually has bread blended up along with walnuts, whereas Georgian walnut sauces do not. This recipe was adapted from the sauce in a recipe for chicken bazhe in *The Georgian Feast* by Darra Goldstein. With toasted spices and a fierce lick of garlic, it's much brighter tasting than its dull color might suggest! **Makes about 1 cup**

1½ teaspoons coriander seeds, or 1 teaspoon ground coriander

½ teaspoon cumin seeds, or ¼ teaspoon ground cumin

1½ cups walnuts

3 or 4 large, or 4 or 5 smaller, garlic cloves, smashed

¾ cup boiling water

2 tablespoons red wine vinegar, plus more if needed

½ teaspoon salt, plus more if needed

¼ teaspoon paprika

½ teaspoon ground marigold or turmeric (optional)

¼ teaspoon black pepper

¼ teaspoon cayenne pepper

If using whole coriander and cumin seeds, toast them in a dry pan over high heat, shaking the pan or stirring frequently, for 1 to 2 minutes, until very fragrant. Immediately transfer to a spice grinder and pulse several times until ground.

In a food processor, combine the walnuts and garlic and process into a smooth paste, stopping to scrape down the sides of the bowl once or twice. Transfer the mixture to a large bowl. While stirring, slowly drizzle in the boiling water. Stir in the vinegar, coriander, cumin, salt, paprika, marigold (if using), black pepper, and cayenne. Taste for seasoning and add more salt, if desired. The sauce can be kept, refrigerated, for up to one week.

# quick-pickled carrot, onion, and radishes

Whether you're popping an Indonesian-style chicken satay off its skewers (page 63) or making your way through a board of charcuterie and cheeses, these simple pickled vegetables are the punchy, crunchy bites you want to eat in between mouthfuls savory, greasy stuff. Refreshing and universal, these pickles can be made with other slivered vegetables, like celery, beets, kohlrabi, sunchokes—pretty much anything you can slice thinly. A mandoline is helpful for making the slices uniformly thin, speeding up the process. **Makes about 2 cups**

1 medium red onion, thinly sliced

1 medium carrot, thinly sliced

2 or 3 radishes, thinly sliced

1 cup rice vinegar

½ cup water

½ cup sugar

1 teaspoon whole black peppercorns

1 bay leaf

½ to 1 teaspoon red chile flakes (optional)

Place the onion, carrot, and radishes in a small heatproof bowl. In a small saucepan, combine the vinegar, water, sugar, peppercorns, bay leaf, and chile flakes (if using) and bring just to a boil over medium high heat, stirring to dissolve the sugar. Pour the brine over the sliced vegetables to submerge them. Let the vegetables cool completely before serving. They can be refrigerated for up to 1 month.

# crispy chile oil

If you've converted to spicy chile crisp cultdom thanks to Lao Gan Ma, a brand of the spicy, crunchy condiment with a dour-faced woman on its label, it's time to make it from scratch. When chile flakes, garlic, and shallots have just sweltered in hot oil, the toasty, spicy, salty flavors are on another level, and a little goes a long way. Try it out in the recipe for Bang Bang Crispy Chicken on page 27, where it's stretched out with vinegar and soy sauce, or just make a fresh batch whenever you're cooking something that can use a kick (every day?). I like to make this chile oil using the simple pour-over method; just be certain to use a vessel that's heatproof up to 500°F. Bakeware such as Pyrex and CorningWare is fine—but whatever you do, don't use just any random glass, as it will shatter (you can use a pot or pan, if you're nervous or unsure). **Makes about ½ cup**

1 small shallot, sliced as thinly as you can (use a mandoline, if it helps)

1 large garlic clove, sliced as thinly as you can (use a mandoline, if it helps)

1 to 2 tablespoons red chile flakes (think 1 for medium heat, 2 for spicy heat)

½ teaspoon salt

½ cup neutral oil, such as grapeseed

Combine the shallot, garlic, chile flakes, and salt in a small heatproof bowl or a large heat-proof measuring cup (or in a small saucepan, if you're unsure if your bowl or measuring cup is heatproof).

Heat the neutral oil in a saucepan over high heat for 2 to 3 minutes, until it is very hot and beginning to smoke. Carefully pour the hot oil over the chile flake mixture, standing away as it bubbles for several seconds. Cool for 10 minutes before using right away. Can be stored, covered in a jar and refrigerated, for up to 3 months.

# kitchen sink chimichurri

I think of chimichurri, a vinegar-brightened, jalapeño-hinted pulse of fresh herbs that originated in South America, as a universal sauce for any kind of grilled or roasted meat. And like pesto, it's a great way to use up leftover half bunches of fresh herbs that are about to wilt. You can be pretty inclusive when it comes to what types of herbs, too. Have a clutch of mint? Bring it on. Parsley, cilantro, and oregano? Add them to the mix. No matter what, it always tastes vibrant, and that's why I consider it my kitchen sink sauce. I'll even throw in the fragrant, feathery tops of carrots or fennel fronds, if they are fresh and tender. You can always skip the jalapeño if you don't feel like adding some heat. **Makes about 2 cups**

3 cups packed leafy fresh herbs, such as cilantro (both leaves and tender stems), parsley, mint, dill, basil, oregano, fennel fronds, or especially young-looking and fragrant carrot greens

2 garlic cloves, minced or grated

½ cup finely chopped onion or shallots

1 jalapeño, seeded and finely chopped (optional)

1 cup extra-virgin olive oil

⅓ cup red wine vinegar, plus more if needed

About ½ teaspoon salt, plus more if needed

¼ teaspoon black pepper, plus more if needed

If you have the time and enjoy hacking away at fresh-smelling herbs on your cutting board (fun and stress-reducing!), mince the herbs by hand and put them in a big bowl. Add the garlic, onion, and jalapeño. Otherwise, combine the herbs, garlic, onion, and jalapeño (if using) in a food processor and pulse several times, stopping to scrape down the sides of the bowl with a spatula. Stir in the olive oil, followed by the vinegar, salt, and pepper. Taste for seasoning and add more vinegar, salt, or pepper as desired. Can be stored in an airtight container in the fridge for 1 week.

# acknowledgments

Chickens are not solitary creatures, and this book was far from a solo effort. I had the great privilege of working with terrific editors across both *TASTE* and Ten Speed: Matt Rodbard, Talia Baiocchi, and Kim Keller. Thanks to Lizzie Munro, photographer, and Pearl Jones, food stylist, for creating such chicken-y masterpieces from these recipes. And to Betsy Stromberg for her creativity with them as the book designer.

Thanks to Lorena Jones, editor in chief at Ten Speed Press, for the opportunity both to write this book and to approach sheet pan chicken from a multicultural perspective. I am so indebted to and inspired by the generous chefs and food writers who contributed a recipe: Melissa Clark, Jenn de la Vega, Von Diaz, Pati Jinich, Yewande Komolafe, Preeti Mistry, Leela Punyaratabandhu, and Louisa Shafia.

To all my friends who helped test-drive and eat chicken recipes, thank you so much for indulging me (and yourselves). To my husband, Olen, for helping me with everything from dishwashing to medical support, like that time I burned all my fingertips.

Thanks to my mom for teaching me not just to eat every grain of rice in my bowl but to suck all the skin and cartilage off the chicken's bones. Thanks to my dad and grandparents for sharing their love of chicken with me as well—often with Cornell sauce. And thanks to all the home cooks I've gotten to know through food and other collaborative events. It makes home cooking much richer and more exciting when you can reference various experiences, conversations, and people with any given dish or ingredient. I'm so grateful to incorporate a grain of salt from everyone I've met.

# index

Copyright © 2020 by Penguin Random House, LLC
Photographs copyright © 2020 by Lizzie Munro

Published in the United States by Ten Speed Press, an imprint of Random House, a division of Penguin Random House LLC, New York.
www.tenspeed.com

Ten Speed Press and the Ten Speed Press colophon are registered trademarks of Penguin Random House LLC.

Grateful acknowledgment is made to the following for permission to reprint previously published material:

Clarkson Potter/Publishers, an imprint of Random House, a division of Penguin Random House LLC and Melissa Clark: "Harissa Chicken with Leeks, Potatoes, and Yogurt" from *Dinner: Changing the Game: A Cookbook* by Melissa Clark, copyright © 2017 by Melissa Clark. Used by permission of Clarkson Potter/Publishers, an imprint of Random House, a division of Penguin Random House LLC, and Melissa Clark.

Pati Jinich: "Oaxacan Chicken with Oregano and Garlic" by Pati Jinich, copyright © 2010–2019 Mexican Table LLC (https://patijinich.com/oaxacan-chicken-with-oregano-and-garlic/). Used by permission of Pati Jinich.

Library of Congress Cataloging-in-Publication Data
    Names: Erway, Cathy, author.
    Title: Sheet pan chicken: 50 simple and satisfying ways to cook dinner / Cathy Erway.
    Description: First edition. | California: Ten Speed Press, [2020] | Includes bibliographical references and index.
    Identifiers: LCCN 2019057940 | ISBN 9781984858542 (hardcover) | ISBN 9781984858559 (epub)
    Subjects: LCSH: Cooking (Chicken) | One-dish meals. | LCGFT: Cookbooks.
    Classification: LCC TX750.5.C45 E79 2020 | DDC 641.6/56–dc23 LC record available at https://lccn.loc.gov/2019057940

Hardcover ISBN: 978-1-9848-5854-2
eBook ISBN: 978-1-9848-5855-9

Printed in China

Design by Betsy Stromberg
Food styling by Pearl Jones

10 9 8 7 6 5 4 3 2 1

First Edition